SINGLE-TRACK MIND

by PAUL SKILBECK

photos of Henrik Djernis by Dave Stewart/Bliss photos
photos of Missy Giove by Tom Moran/Singletrack photos

VELOPRESS • BOULDER, COLORADO

Skilbeck, Paul, 1962-
          Single-track mind / by Paul Skilbeck : photos by Dave Stewart, Tom Moran.
                    p.   cm.
          Includes bibliographical references and index.
          ISBN 1-884737-10-2
          1. All terrain cycling — Training.   I. Title.
GV1056.S55   1996
796.6 — dc20   96-7888
                                                               CIP

PRINTED IN THE USA

VeloPress™
1830 N. 55th Street
Boulder, CO 80301-2700
USA
303/440-0601
FAX 303/444-6788
EMAIL: velonews@aol.com
WEB SITE: http://www.VeloNews.com/VeloNews

TO PURCHASE ADDITIONAL COPIES OF THIS BOOK OR OTHER VELO™ PRODUCTS,
PLEASE CALL 800/234-8356. FOR INTERNATIONAL ORDERS CALL 303/440-0601 EXT. 6

ACKNOWLEDGMENTS

A mixture of circumstances made putting this book together far more difficult than I could have imagined. In the end, I received more help (from a variety of people) than I had any right to ask for. I am hugely grateful to everyone involved with this project, and in particular: the model racers Missy Giove and Henrik Djernis, who gave a lot more time than we initially asked for; Club la Santa, Lanzarote, for providing a base at short notice for the technique shots with Henk; physiologists Dr. Joanne Fallowfield and Trevor Dobbins of the Chichester Institute of Higher Education, who wrote Chapter 13, read several chapters and patiently advised me; the staff at VeloPress, in particular Marti Stephen, Mark Saunders and Michael Sitrin, who went far beyond the call of duty in their work on this project; and most important of all, a heartfelt thanks to my sister, Clare, and all the close friends who said and did exactly the right things at the right time.

Contents

Preface

Mountain biking is still a very new sport. After arriving with a bang in the 1980s, it has continued to attract a phenomenal amount of interest and attention in the 1990s. As a result of mountain biking's growing popularity, there has been an exponential improvement in mountain-bike technology and training techniques.

This book is intended to stay on the cutting edge of these training techniques and continue to play a useful role in the skills development of mountain bike racers and riders. In writing this book, I attempted to fill the huge gap in information created by the rapid growth of mountain biking. The problem is that relatively little scientific research has been conducted about mountain bike training and racing, which makes it difficult to state that a certain type of training is best. However, through the limited data that already exist, it's clear that some riders respond better to particular training technique "A", while other riders respond better to technique "B." For example, shorter, harder rides have proved successful conditioning work for some riders, while longer, easier rides have worked best for others. All riders need to combine the two, with the addition of some skills work as well. The problem to be solved is finding the right balance for you.

Physiologists and coaches can make accurate measurements and give reasoned advice to help you reach your goals, but even they do not have all the answers — they are just better skilled at interpreting data and making educated guesses. The purpose of this book is to assemble the best theories currently available about mountain bike training and racing, and present them in an easy-to-understand format. My advice is to use the exercises in this book to find out what works best for you and go on from there. Remember: A thousand-mile journey begins with the first step.

As with any continuing project, feedback is important. I welcome feedback and comments from anyone who reads this book.

Introduction

The book

First and foremost, mountain biking is an adventure. It has the almost universal effect of making people of all ages shriek with excitement. Most importantly, mountain biking takes people on a journey in which they learn a lot about themselves, other people and the planet we live on. In this way, mountain biking can be rewarding, as well as great fun. For many, the adventure of mountain biking leads to racing. And it is for racers that I have written this book; although, anyone who wants to become fitter, or learn more about riding a mountain bike, will benefit from reading this book.

Unfortunately, there is a shortage of scientific studies about mountain bike racing; therefore, much of the material in this book comes from qualitative, rather than quantitative, sources. In other words, much of the information comes from simple observation of pro riders and my own first-hand experiences. At this stage in the sport's development, I do not see this lack of scientific data as a weakness. In fact, my hope is that this book serves as a ground-breaker for scientific research in the field of mountain biking.

In these early years of mountain bike racing, individual and group case studies of riders are the most valuable training indicators at our disposal. These observations, coupled with the relevant aspects of human physiology, and tempered with common sense, form a reasonable and functional approach to mountain-bike training theory. This is the approach taken in *Single-Track Mind*.

TRAINING

If you are taking the time and trouble to train, it's important to remember that every minute of exercise results in some kind of psychological and physiological adjustment. The question for all athletes is, "Are all of these adjustments really helping?" In the case of a mountain bike racer, "Are these adjustments helping you win races?" If your training is not tailored for your particular needs, then, at least to some degree, you're wasting your time and energy, and possibly doing yourself some damage as well. This book is designed to help you identify what kind of training you need throughout the entire year.

While you're planning your season, it's important to remember that mountain bike training is not just about physical conditioning. In addition, a successful mountain bike racer must develop the following: bike-handling skills (and a knowledge of how to apply them to a wide range of ground conditions); tactical elements (such as pacing and the ability to read other riders); and a winning mindset that separates you from the rest of the field.

If this sounds like a lot, you're on the right track. Any newcomer to mountain bike racing should allow a minimum of three full seasons to grasp the wide range of skills, conditioning and nuances involved in the sport. When you consider that mountain bike racing combines the endurance of marathon running with the finesse of slalom skiing, it's a lot to take on. This book will guide you toward becoming a better mountain bike rider and racer.

As you train for mountain bike racing, you'll find that it can be tough. That's why the credo of this book is *if something is a skill, then it can be learned and improved upon with the right practice*. It is as simple as that. This book will help you to identify what you need to learn, and it will provide a framework for improving a wide array of skills. After that, it's largely up to you.

Training plans

A good training plan should assist your decisions, but remain flexible enough to be fine-tuned daily, weekly or monthly, if necessary. If you decide to fine-tune your training program, this decision to do so should be founded on a solid base of knowledge about you as a rider and supported by rationale. In other words, it's always better to know than to guess. After all, who wants to go around stabbing away in the dark?

Using this book

Some readers will want to dive into particular chapters, others will want to read it from beginning to end. I have tried to accommodate both approaches. The earlier chapters (1 to 5) deal with more basic information, including some basic physiology and principles of fitness and training. It has been my experience that even advanced riders can benefit from this information. The middle chapters (6 to11) deal with the components of training, which include psychological and organizational matters, as well as structuring a training program. The latter chapters (12 to 16) are on riding skills. No matter how you tackle this book the first time around, I hope that after a year or two, it will have several well-thumbed and grungy pages.

Chapter 1

Position on the bike

Not so long ago, a good riding position meant your feet could touch the ground without your top tube inflicting serious pain, allowing your parents the peace of mind that you wouldn't fall over when stopping at the end of the driveway. Times have changed. Today, a good position gets you up a mountain swiftly and back down safely. Without the correct riding position, you will not receive the full benefits of any training program. Worse yet, an incorrect riding positon could lead to injury. In that respect, some things never change. In any event, if you were thinking about skipping this chapter because your bike already fits you fine, I strongly urge you to reconsider and read on.

The first thing to do when evaluating your riding position is ask yourself honestly, "is my position as good as it could be?" In terms of bike set-up, the difference between a good position and a mediocre one is tiny, often fractions of an inch. In terms of the way it feels, it's gigantic. A good riding position not only broadens the scope of your mountain biking activities, it also enables you to go between A and B in less time using the same amount of energy. This is because a good position does three things: it promotes efficiency in energy transfer from your muscles to the pedals; provides a position that is conducive to being balanced in all situations; and enables you to be comfortable on your bike. By contrast, a poor riding position renders you more prone to accidents and injuries, and is less energy efficient.

This chapter explores different approaches to, and reasons for, setting up bikes for cross-country and downhill, and the effects of set-up on bike handling. Before I elaborate, remember that set-up varies greatly between downhill and cross-country. What works best for one involves a big compromise for the other. If you're devoted to only one discipline, it's still useful to read about the set-up for the other. You can never know too much about this subject.

THE DIFFERENCE BETWEEN DOWNHILL AND CROSS-COUNTRY POSITIONS
Downhill

Downhill racing requires a low seat and relatively high handlebars, thereby lowering the rider's center of gravity even though the position is slightly more upright. The lower center of gravity gives more stability in corners, and raising the handlebars makes it easier to get the front wheel off the ground on a steep descent.

A good downhill position, like a race-horse jockey's position, looks cramped and ungainly when riding to the starting line, but out on the course it is the only way to go. Although the abbreviated leg extension sacrifices pedaling efficiency, full compensation is rewarded in the extra bike-handling potential offered by a lower center of gravity. Let's look at a case in point.

In a moment of pre-race jitters before the 1995 World Cup downhill race at Big Bear, California, Regina Stiefl of Germany (the eventual 1995 Grundig World Cup downhill series winner), forgot to lower her saddle after warming up and started the race with it several inches higher than normal. "I was too nervous to notice it at the starting gate, but in the first corner I realized my mistake," she said. The course, which resembled an over-sized BMX track, was ideally suited to Stiefl's powerful, flowing style. Instead of coming in first, she finished tenths of a second behind U.S. rider Elke Brutsaert.

At the finish, Stiefl was surprised that she had done so well. She felt she hadn't had a good run. I must stress that the course permitted her to benefit from an improved pedaling stroke while seated, and sprinting out of corners can be accomplished very effectively from the standing position, regardless of seat height. Still, with her seat up too high, she was simply unable to get low enough in the corners, particularly in the off-camber sections.

One possible exception to all this is Mammoth Mountain's

DO I NEED TWO BIKES?

The specialization of mountain-bike design need not be a big financial deterrent to the all-rounder. At the international level, a specialist bike is important, but at all levels beneath international competition, it isn't necessary to purchase a specialist cross-country or downhill bike. Several manufacturers make full-suspension bikes that are suitable for both cross-country and downhill racing. You might note that it is more usual to see a cross-country bike being raced in a downhill event than the other way around; however, this is probably because it's more difficult to convert a downhill bike to cross-country use than vice versa — and a downhill bike is usually heavier. Also notice that Henrik Djernis's cross-country bike (1.1) is almost indistinguishable from Missy Giove's downhill bike (1.2).

Notice how the handlebars on a downhill bike (1.2) are closer to the seat and higher up than on a cross-country bike. A downhill bike also has a longer wheelbase. Cross-country bikes (1.1) typically have a wheelbase in the range of 41 to 42 inches, while downhill bikes can have a 45-inch wheelbase or even longer.

famous Kamikaze downhill. The highest unofficial course speed is 67 mph, recorded in 1989 by British racer David Baker, riding a fully rigid cross-country bike. He probably still has nightmares about that ride today. Anyway, Baker finished seventh in the race, mainly because his biggest chainring (only 46 teeth) was inadequate on the lower section; however, the lower handlebars of his cross-country position gave Baker an aerodynamic advantage more so than higher, wider downhill bars would have. It is possible to get away with low, narrow handlebars on the Kamikaze, but on almost all other courses the higher, wider handlebar position is the one to adopt — more on that later.

Cross-Country

Cross-country racers have entirely different needs from the downhill crowd — in fact opposite needs: a higher seat and low handlebars. The body position created by this configuration puts more weight on the front wheel. This is particularly important on steep climbs, where weighting the front wheel is a key factor in steering control. Linked to this is the matter of labored breathing. You have to make it easy to breathe deeply. The "longer" cross-country position stretches the torso, allowing the lungs to expand and fill with air with a minimum of resistance. Another reason that cross-country bars need to be so low

is that this position lowers the rider's center of gravity; however, there is a limit to how low to go, which is explained later in **Setting Up Your Bike**.

Overall, the cross-country position trades a bit of handling potential for a lot of extra pedal power.

DIFFERENT BY DESIGN

The design of downhill and cross-country bikes reflects the different ways that the two types of riding have developed, and the different demands each type makes on the rider. Pictures 1.1 and 1.2 show two bikes that might look similar to the casual observer; however, if you rode both of these bikes, it would feel like you were visiting two different planets — each one interacts with the ground in a completely different way. Sure, they both have front and rear suspension, but so what? Very soon, cross-country racers will wonder how they ever managed without front and rear suspension. The features that differentiate these bikes are the distance of suspension travel; the design and geometry of the frame; the strength of the wheels; the gearing; the overall weight of the bike — and so on.

Whereas most cross-country bikes have a similar wheelbase, measured from the center of the front hub to the center of the rear hub, downhill bikes exhibit considerable variation. Some have a foreshortened wheelbase for tight, technical courses on which the main advantages to such a bike are agility through the turns and acceleration out of them. The notorious World Cup downhill course at Cap d'Ail, France, is a perfect example of this type of course. The dual-slalom event is also appropriate for a foreshortened wheelbase. On the other hand, a long wheel base is an advantage on faster courses. Mammoth Mountain's Kamikaze downhill course is ideal for these bikes. Having said that, we should remember that in 1995 Missy Giove won the Grundig World Cup downhill race at Cap d'Ail riding the long-wheelbase Cannondale bike pictured on the previous page, proving that ultimately the victory belongs to the rider, not the bike.

THE FIRST STEP

The first thing you should do when you get a new bike, or change something on your existing bike, is write down the exact measurements. It can take quite a while to arrive at a position that really suits you, and you should record your progress along the way. The advantage of this is that once you've hit perfection, you have it down on paper as well. If you experiment a bit, you may create a new position that is not so popular with your limbs and torso. In that case, you'd better have your previous measurements written down, so you can restore them.

Even after you have found the "perfect" position, further changes might become necessary. Advances in technology could make it desirable to make a major alteration to your bike. In particular, I'm thinking about suspension and the different approaches there are to that. The thing is, if you've taken the essential measurements before the additon of a suspension fork, you can still set up your bike to give your body a position similar to what made you happy in the first place.

The essential measurements to record are listed below and in Diagram 1.3.

To make these measurements use a spirit level and steel ruler.

① Horizontal distance from hadlebars to nose of seat.

② Vertical distance from handlebars to nose of seat.

③ Horizontal distance from nose of seat to crank axle.

④ Distance, in line with seat tube, from top of seat to center of crank axle.

⑤ The dimensions and angles of your frame.

THE VAGARIES OF POSITION

One common formula about handlebar position suggests that the handlebars are in the right position when they obscure the front hub while the rider is in the normal seated position. This formula may have some application to road bikes, but it does not apply to mountain biking. Mountain bike handlebars are normally ahead of the line of vision to the front hub. But that said, I do not agree with the idea of trying to fit the vast array of human body shapes and riding styles into hard and fast formulas.

For example, this notion that handlebars should obscure the front hub does not account for riders with a relatively long or short neck or torso. As for pedaling action, Jacques Anquetil was a toes-down rider, Eddy Merckx a heels-down rider, and both are five-time winners of the Tour de France. The complexities in the biomechanics of pedaling are mind boggling. Believe me, I've discussed the task analysis of pedaling with ergonomics experts and concluded that by far the most effective solution is to adopt a position which *you* feel gives you the most efficiency and balance. So what if it looks unusual? If it works for you, then do it. If in doubt about where to start, try to approximate the positions of Henk Djernis and Missy Giove. Ask an experienced rider from your local cycling club, but watch out for old wives' tales and formulas taken from road cycling. The rule of thumb when asking for advice about riding position is that the more certain a rider is of his or her theory, the less likely it is to be correct.

Take these measurements carefully and always use the same equipment and procedure each time. Record these dimensions, along with the date of each measurement, in a ring binder or similar notebook. I recommend using a training diary such as the *VeloNews* training diary. Over the years, as you move from bike to bike, you will find these additional records an invaluable reference for position analysis and making decisions about changes.

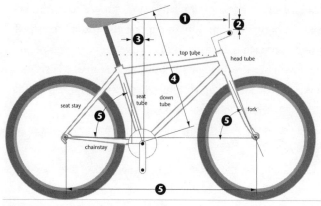

DIAGRAM 1.3

SETTING UP YOUR BIKE

Even though there is a wide range of differences between the positions for cross-country and downhill bikes, I want to mention that common ground is found between them in the position of the rider's foot and knee in relation to the pedal. Leg positioning is critical to the production of power.

You should try to get this adjustment pin perfect, because of the huge number of pedal strokes you make in a race. If your pedaling position is even a tiny bit inefficient, it makes a difference each time you push on the pedals. Over time, this has a major effect, particularly when your legs start to get tired. Okay, so there are substantially fewer pedal strokes in downhill than in cross-country, but don't forget that in downhill you apply nearly maximum effort, and therefore each pedal stroke counts for more.

Seat tilt

When setting your seat position, you can waste a lot of time if you don't get the sequence of adjustments in the right order. The first thing you have to do is choose the tilt of your seat. It is universally standard to have a level seat, but some people choose to tilt the nose down. This tends to thrust your weight forward, which means more pressure on the palms of your hands. If you're tilting your seat forward to relieve pressure on

the crotch, remember that seats with a small cut-out are available, and help to relieve pressure on the perineum. You'll especially want to avoid tilting the seat nose up because this can cause injury and numbness in this area. It is sufficient to check the tilt of your seat just with your eyes; a spirit level isn't really needed.

Feet on pedals

This is relatively easy. Regardless of your shoe size, the important thing is to have the ball of your foot centered over the pedal axle. You may need an Allen key, or possibly even a screwdriver, to adjust the cleats to achieve this.

The next part gets slightly more complicated, but don't worry; if you take care and go over it slowly, you'll get it right. It begins with seat height, which differs with each discipline, so I shall separate discussions here.

SEAT HEIGHT

Downhill

For the best power generation, a downhiller needs to get his/her knee vertically over the pedal axle, but the precise height of the seat should depend on the course. Tighter curves, steeper drops and technical terrain mean a lower seat. Missy Goive, for example, chooses a seat height between four and seven inches lower than on her cross-country bike, depending on the course.

Moving the seat within a three-inch range will affect the position of your knee over the pedal axle. Now find your neutral pedal position using the procedure on page 13. If you put markers on your seat rails corresponding with markers on your seatpost (with indelible pen, don't file notches, whatever you do), you can adjust your seat fore and aft in concert with height adjustments. It is a very simple operation.

Setting up the seat height will always be a compromise. What you gain in control, you lose in power. These days, it is important to be good at pedaling and bike control, so don't succumb to the temptation to specialize in one or the other. This means you should think about setting your seat height at a level that enables you to be good at both.

When it comes to training, however, feel free to do most of your hard physical work with your seat at cross-country height, or road height if, like Missy, you do road workouts. If you ride only in the low position you risk serious damage to your knees. For successful downhill racing, it is more important to develop good aerobic power and good lactate tolerance than it is to

NEUTRAL PEDAL POSITION

Your seat height will change with each discipline. You will have to find the neutral pedal position for each height. To find your netural pedal position, you will need the following equipment:
• a plumb line (lightweight string with a weight at the bottom).
• someone to help you take measurements.
• a turbo trainer (or similar).
• an Allen key to slide seat fore and aft on its rails.
• a ruler and spirit level to take measurements.

The neutral pedaling position involves the front of your knee pushing down on the pedal axle in a vertical line, when the cranks are at the horizontal position. When you measure it, your foot absolutely must be in its normal pedaling position at this point, because if the heel is raised or lowered from your normal posi-

tion, your knee will react to this new position, and that will defeat the purpose of the measurements.

To begin, set your bike up in the turbo trainer and pedal until you are confident that your foot will rest in its normal pedaling position when you stop for a measurement. When you are ready, your helper runs the plumb line down the side of your leg from the indentation between the femur and kneecap to the axle. The plumb line can't go over the front of your leg because some people have very knobby knees. The point is to measure from the forward extremity of the femur, not your kneecap. If you think it will help, mark this spot on your leg with a pen when you find it. Your helper then dangles the line to see where it falls, then adjusts your seat forward or back until the plumb line bisects your pedal axle.

Now you have the neutral position.

Your helper tightens the seat bolt before you do anything else, then you climb off and run the plumb line down from the nose of the seat past the bottom bracket spindle. Using the spirit level to make sure the ruler is horizontal, measure the distance between the bottom bracket spindle and plumb line. This is important.

The next thing to do is make a fine adjustment, if any are required. As a very general rule — and one that you could be justified in ignoring — downhillers move beyond the neutral pedaling position so that the plumb line, from the nose of the saddle, falls about half an inch in front of the bottom-bracket axle. Cross-country riders normally keep it centered, but some like it up to an inch behind the axle.

develop super-strong quads.

Cross-Country

Most pro mountain bikers adopt a slightly lower seat height on their mountain bikes than on their road bikes. This is because of factors such as the increased bike-handling demands of mountain biking and the need to dismount-remount. Normally, a mountain bike's seat height is within one inch of that on the road bike.

Finding your correct seat height is a bit difficult. I'm not really one to recommend a formula for this. I'm sorely tempted to advise you to adopt something that feels comfortable and capable of delivering good power to the pedals.

Look, how about this: Put your bike back in the turbo trainer and call your helper back. Take off your shoes and socks and climb on your bike. Put your heels on the pedals and start ped-

aling. Ask your helper to stand behind you and see if your pelvis is rocking as you pedal, or if it stays calm and motionless. If it's the former, your seat is probably too high. It should be that as your pedal passes the point farthest from your seat, your heel almost loses contact with it; all the while your pelvis should remain majestically calm.

Once you have found this seat height, you will possibly need to alter its fore and aft adjustment. Again, find your neutral pedal position and mark your spots. The reason for this re-adjustment is because the seat tube is tilted, not vertical, so altering your seat height also alters the lateral distance from your knee to the line of your pedal axle.

If you can't get along with the seat height that results from the above experiment, feel free to change it to where it feels better.

1.4

BODY POSITION

Downhill

Downhill riders tend toward a relatively upright position, achieved by a lower seat and a short stem that angles upward. You won't go too wrong emulating the basic set-up of Missy's bike in Figure 1.4.

The upright position of her Cannondale DH Super V allows Missy to unweight the front wheel more easily. The main effect of a short handlebar stem is to create a relatively compact position on the bike. You can see this in Figure 1.4. Compare this to Henk in Figure 1.5. Missy's elbows are relatively close to her waist. With this more compact position, the bike tends to be more sensitive to changes in body position.

Figures 1.6, 1.7 and 1.8 illustrate the range of positions a downhill rider needs to adopt over the course of a downhill run. When it gets fast'n'funky there is no such thing as over-exaggerating body position.

PEDALING ACTION

Because every aspect of the pedal stroke is important, your pedaling action deserves to come under the magnifying glass. Correct ankle rotation and leg-muscle coordination are the keys to an efficient stroke.

To really get a feel for this, you need to put your bike on a turbo trainer and take one foot out of the pedal. Turn the cranks with the other foot and you will quickly appreciate where your major and minor flat spots are. The wonderful thing about this exercise is that it teaches you to push forward through the top of the pedal stroke, then start pulling back even before your foot has reached the bottom of the cycle.

Another good exercise is to pedal downhill in your middle or granny ring. Keep your upper body still and ride a straight line while pedaling at 150 plus rpm. (The trick to this is being rhythmical, applying power only in the first third of each revolution. Also, use less ankle rotation than at lower revolution rates.)

The most esoteric, and arguably most important, thing about pedaling is what the French (and cyclists from many other nations) call *souplesse*. Literally translated it means "suppleness." In cycling parlance, it tends to mean a bit more than that. It relates to turning the pedals with a feeling of ease and smoothness. The best way to feel *souplesse* is when riding in the saddle up a climb, preferably a steep one where you are putting your back into it. First, stop putting your back into it, and let your legs do the work. Allow the leg movement to end at the place your hip inserts into your pelvis and just enjoy that feeling of a still pelvis, a relaxed upper body, and hard-working legs. The result is a smoother ride and less strain on the lower back muscles. All of the pros pedal this way, and if you are ever in doubt about how your foot and ankle should work on the bike, go back to the one-footed pedaling exercise.

If you're still not convinced, I should point out that the place where good pedaling style really comes into play is on very steep, technical climbs, where any pull on the handlebars immediately results in a loss of control.

The compact position Missy has on her downhill bike enables her to stretch a long way back over the rear wheel (Figure 1.8) by straightening her arms, bending her knees and pushing back. She loses a lot of front wheel control in doing this, but it helps to lower her center of gravity. When the combined center of gravity of the bike and rider passes forward of the front axle on a steep descent, the rider normally takes a tumble over the handlebars. The opposite is the case with wheelies and the rear axle.

Missy's position in Figure 1.8 serves a very different purpose than in Figure 1.7. Here she is in the speed tuck. Her weight is well forward, where it needs to be to keep the front wheel tracking as she grabs a fistful of front brake.

When not braking, she would enhance the aerodynamic effect of the speed tuck by drawing her knees in close to the frame tubes. In Figure 1.7, she has transferred new weight over the back wheel to prevent going over the bars on this short, steep descent.

Cross-Country

For racing, you can't go too wrong by emulating Henk's position in 1.5. In order to arrive at this position, you'll need a frame with a long top tube if you have a long torso, and vice versa for a short torso. Physiologists, statisticians and framebuilders have told me that women tend to have relatively shorter torsos than men. In mountain biking, this is certainly not a big problem, because several companies make frames with female customers in mind.

BIKE SET-UP
Downhill

Setting up your downhill bike so that it avoids flats is another major consideration. The most common type of flat is the pinch-flat (often called "snake bike" because of the two holes the rim leaves in the tube). One of the best ways to avoid this is to use tire liners of some sort and run a tire pressure of at least 35 pounds per square inch (psi).

Front disc brakes have a lot of appeal because of their stopping power, but the torque they create makes them best suited to forks with a triple crown. A good example of a triple crown is a Gyrvin fork (See Henk's bike).

MISSY'S TIPS FOR DOWNHILL BIKE SET-UP

① Get a strong set of rims.
② Tires with thick sidewalls help avoid pinch flats.
③ A full-suspension bike is not absolutely necessary.
④ Get a chain-retention device for the chainrings. You can make your own by cutting a Manitou bumper in half and zip-tying it to the front derailleur, or you can buy one.
⑤ Put a quick release on your seatpost. Sometimes you might need a higher seat, and it's a lot easier than carrying a wrench.
⑥ Get a stem that is not too long or stretched out and gives a good rise.
⑦ If converting a cross-country bike, use riser handlebars. You should be okay with flat bars on a downhill frame. Whatever bars you get, make sure they are extra strong. There is less risk of them snapping, and they don't need to be replaced as often.
⑧ If you're serious about downhill and shorter than 5 feet 8 inches tall consider using 170mm cranks, not 175mm. I use this crank length on all my bikes, including my road bike.

With handlebars, go as wide as you can stand. Slightly wider than shoulder width is a good solution. As for height, this depends a bit on the course. There is no need to adjust your bars as much as your seat. Without seeing how you look on your bike, it is hard for me to say exactly what height to choose. A good place to start experimenting is by setting your bars level with your seat when it's set at its highest downhill position.

Whether you like it or not, you will have to learn to be an authority on suspension. I could fill this entire book with the fine points of setting up suspension. As it is, I'm no expert in this field, so my advice is to get out there and start experimenting for yourself. Almost all suspension systems are designed to be tuned, and different courses demand different compression, return and damping rates. The best way to start learning about all these things is to keep notes about what you have done and what the result was. It is no good to rely on the expertise of friends. After all, only you know exactly how your bike responds to you and your riding style.

Cross-Country
Top tube

Top-tube length is important, because if the handlebar stem is too short or too long to make up for deficiencies in the top tube's length, then the handling is adversely affected. And after all that careful adjustment of the seat for the proper pedaling position, you wouldn't adjust the seat for the sake of torso fit, would you?

Stem length

Given the correct top tube-length, a handlebar stem in the range of 110mm to 140mm delivers the best steering response in a variety of uphill and downhill conditions. Shorter than this, and the front end starts to get a bit light on steep climbs; longer, and you are too far forward on the steep descents.

Stem height

Looking at Figure 1.1, you can see that Henk's bike has a pretty fair drop from the nose of the seat to the handlebars. This is a good amount of drop for him because it allows Henk to get enough weight down and forward without placing too much strain on his back, shoulders and neck. If he were to lower his handlebars, even by an inch he would probably start to suffer from pain in his lumbar spine, shoulders and neck.

Personally, I like a position similar to Henk's, but I know it's not for everybody. If you're aiming for a more upright position, try to make sure that your back is straight and that you aren't bunched up into a cramped posture. Not only does a straight back look a lot better, it's much better for your breathing on the bike, and in the long term, the health of your spine.

The cheapest way to achieve a more upright position is with a higher-rise stem. If you buy one of these, make sure it maintains the same distance to the nose of your seat as the 110mm to 140mm stem I mentioned above.

Bar width and bar ends

Although some riders like a very narrow bar, none of the pros do. This useless modification throws off your bike-handling ability. It is more common to have your bars fractionally wider than your shoulder width. By the time you have mounted your bar ends, you have a position fractionally narrower than shoulder width — which is as narrow as you'd want to go.

The tilt of the bar ends is mainly a matter of taste. One argument is that bar ends are used mainly when you stand up, so they should be almost horizontal, which creates a more comfortable line between wrist and forearm. I suggest about one to one-and-a-half inches of rise (about 10 to 15 degrees), which makes them comfortable in most situations.

RECREATIONAL POSITION

For recreational riding I would opt for a more upright position. You are better able to negotiate bumps in the trail, and you have better all-around vision. The thing to remember with the more upright position is to put a lot of weight on the front wheel on fast corners. The danger of not doing this is that the tire will lose traction and wash out sideways. So you start to see that body position not only affects breathing, vision and weight bearing, but steering as well.

GENERAL NOTE

It can easily take a year or two of experimenting until you find a position that you feel is really good for you. So, juniors are at the greatest advantage in finding a good position, because the younger you are when you start to analyze your riding position, the less your cycling career is likely to be hindered by bad posture and pedaling inefficiencies. The disadvantage juniors have is that they are changing shape all the time, and during growth spurts they must check their positions about once a month to see if they are still right.

We all have different body shapes and muscle-fiber mixtures; therefore, I don't like to make general statements about the best position on a bike. One thing I can say without fear of being wrong is that no one formula exists that will be suitable for everyone.

Your bike's set-up is also linked to your performance. So, keep in mind that adjustments should be made slowly to allow your body to start functioning at its peak in a new position. If you decide that you need to raise your seat height by an inch, make four adjustments over the course of two weeks, instead of a single adjustment.

We've gone into depth about the differences between cross-country and downhill bikes on the basis of control. The next chapter will examine the basics of control and begin to take this show off road.

Chapter 2

The basics of control

Now that your bike is set up to give you the most efficient riding position, it's time to get into the basics of off-road technique. In practice, riding technique is a series of bike-handling skills strung together, and no matter how bad your skills are now, they can be improved — sometimes overnight.

There are eight basic bike-handling skills: braking, gear selection, steering and cornering, fore-aft movement and bunny-hops, grip, basic jumping, the neutral position and mental maps. Once you have mastered these basic skills, there is no limit to what you can do on a mountain bike.

As with any physical activity, mountain biking relies heavily on your senses. The three main senses used in mountain biking are vision, touch and hearing. Balance is also very important, though it's not really a sense. Balance is your ability to orient yourself in space, which comes from a combination of sensory input (vision and touch) and the movement-control systems in your inner ear.

VISION

Vision is the most important sense to a mountain bike racer. The position of your head and direction of your vision determines the direction of your bike: You go where your eyes go. In other words, the best way to avoid hitting that big rock in the middle of the trail is to look past it. This advice not only applies to rocks, but to ditches, drop-offs, water ... you name it. Next time you are at a race, notice how relaxed and matter-of-fact pro riders are about not staring at the obstacles they're trying to avoid. Note the direction of Henk's gaze in Figures 2.1-3.

To ride like the pros, there are two basic rules to improve your

As Henk approaches an outcrop of rocks sprawling across a narrow corner, he chooses his line early and keeps focused on it. Although these small rocks wouldn't throw him, their sharp edges could easily cause a pinch flat. In the final frame of the sequence, after setting himself up to pass safely through the gap, Henk moves his attention to the next obstacle.

Henk is out of the seat as he passes over some bumps on the trail. This is the classic downhill position, also used as the "ready" position in cross-country. From here he can tackle just about anything, or merely give his tail a rest from the rigors of the trail.

vision: keep your head up and continually scan the trail in front of you to see what's coming. Unless you are in a technical section that requires closer attention to detail, it's a good idea to keep your eyes focused between 15 and 50 feet in front of you; this way, you can see what's coming and get out of the way of any potential problems. You aren't staring at your front wheel watching the rocks go by either, which is a common rookie mistake and a sure-fire way to make yourself crash. Another thing to watch out for is riding at dusk or when the light is flat. In both situations, obstacles like boulders and trail gates start to blend into the trail. This can make descending a little dicey.

Of course, you aren't constantly scanning the trail ahead of you. Occasionally, you'll want to glance down at the cycle-computer and heart-rate monitor displays on your handlebars, or it might be necessary to glance at a part of your bike if something isn't working right. The idea is simple: Pay close attention to the terrain in front of you.

German downhill champion Jurgen Beneke says that he has trained his eyes to focus five meters and 50 meters ahead, both at the same time. Missy concurs with this, and adds, "It depends on what's ahead. If it's a non-technical course, like the Kamikaze, I'm going to look a lot farther ahead. But on a course like Mont-Sainte-Anne, you can't focus a long way ahead and just roll over what's beneath you, because you'd crash."

TOUCH

On a mountain bike, tactile feedback comes through your hands, your butt and your feet. This sensory feedback keeps you in control and on top of the bike, as opposed to the other

way around. Beginners and out-of-control riders experience this feedback as if they were on top of a bucking stallion, but as your bike-handling skills improve, the ride becomes more smooth and you start to feel "light" on the bike. This change happens because now you're moving with the bike as it encounters obstacles, instead of merely hanging on for dear life. Moving with the bike translates into making frequent adjustments (backwards-and-forwards, side-to-side, up-and-down) that allow you to stay in harmony with the bike's movement.

When your timing is off, tactile feedback (in the form of jolts and bumps) will quickly let you know it's time to make corrections. Perfecting your timing on a mountain bike is all about rhythm and anticipation. In a way, you can compare mountain biking to ballet dancing. Instead of making a series of staccato movements to the rhythm of the beat, a ballet dancer moves fluidly through a variety of complicated movements, right in time with the music. The same applies to mountain bike riding. Obviously, the beat of the trail is less regular than most musical rhythms, but the dance between bike and rider still has to be choreographed. When you ride in sync with your bike, you become your own natural shock absorber.

Missy moving at moderate speed. This is the downhiller's "ready" position. Again, you can see how much more compact and upright it is than the cross-country posture. From this position, she is able to react the most quickly to obstacles on the trail.

If you momentarily lose your rhythm, your elbows and knees can absorb some pretty big hits; however, your rear end cannot. Big jolts up through the saddle transmit too much shock to the spine. The best way to avoid this is to stand up when the going gets rough. By transferring your weight to your hands and feet, you free up your entire body to act as a giant shock absorber. A common misconception about fully suspended bikes is that you can remain seated all the time. You can stay

seated a lot more than you could on a front-suspensions only bike — which saves a lot of energy over the course of a race — but you still have to stand up when the downhill terrain gets rough. This is clearly demonstrated by both Missy and Henk in Figures 2.4 and 2.5.

HEARING

Hearing may be the least important of the three senses used in mountain biking, but it is still vital to your success. Unless you plan on looking over your shoulder all the time, which is hard to do in the middle of a race, listening is the only way to tell what's going on behind you.

You also have to know how to respond to your bike when it starts making unusual noises. These noises indicate that something is wrong with your bike. Sometimes unusual noises are just annoying (like a misaligned derailleur), but they often indicate that something is seriously wrong — like the hiss a tire makes when it is going flat, which may give you enough time to slow down before the tire parts company with the rim. I don't need to tell you how helpful that kind of advance warning can be.

Regardless of the source of the noise, knowing how to respond to the different noises your bike makes is crucial. It could even save your life.

2.6 *Henk has risen slightly off the seat in the final few meters before a sharp rise. His knees and elbows are flexed and ready to start pedaling.*

2.7 *Henk has moved forward and his knees have extended, pushing his hips up. His forward movement keeps his weight centered over the bike, while pulling up on the bars and down with his hips, keeps Henk from flossing his teeth with the front tire.*

2.8 *Henk continues to extend his knees as the bike nears the top. In this way he's working with it to crest the rise. He hasn't pedaled now for about 10 yards. The approach Henk takes with this move is to clear this obstacle with finesse, not power.*

2.9 *With the bike now atop the rise, Henk starts to move back, staying centered over the bike.*

2.10 *Even though the gradient is not severe enough to cause Henk to lean back over the rear wheel, he is leaning back behind the saddle. Note that even his shoulders have moved back.*

2.11 *Approaching the bottom of the slope, Henk starts to move forward again. He's still centered on the bike, as has been his purpose throughout the exercise.*

THE NEUTRAL POSITION

A good mountain-bike riding position is different from a good road-bike position. This is because road riders tend to spend a lot of time in one or two positions, while mountain bikers move all over the bike as the terrain changes. Henk demonstrated the seated neutral position in Chapter 1, Figure 1.5 (notice how relaxed his shoulders, elbows and knees are). In Figure 2.4, he demonstrates the neutral position while standing.

These are the two most versatile positions for cross-country racing. They permit the rider the freedom to move quickly into a variety of other positions that a mountain-bike course is likely to demand.

Henk often assumes this standing position on descents, or on bumpy terrain where the bike is going to jump around beneath him. On jagged terrain, Henk's front suspension takes the edge off the bumps, but your best suspension comes from having supple arms and legs. If your shoulders, elbows and knees are stiff and rigid, the bike will be much harder to control.

GEARS

What follows is a general description of which gears to use to fit the terrain.

Front cogs

• Big ring — Downhill; fast flat terrain; short steep climbs; gradual climbs if you feel very strong and want to stand up on the pedals (not energy efficient, but a good way of relieving tired muscles). Racers occasionally use the big ring on flat terrain with small, high-frequency bumps because it's easier to pedal at a lower cadence, and sometimes it's easier to pedal in the big ring while standing, rather than staying seated and using a middle-ring gear.

• Middle ring — The most-used chainring. It's for slow flat terrain, or when you don't want to hammer; technical or slower downhills; easy-to-moderate climbs; and short steep climbs.

• Inner (small) ring or granny gear — Long steep climbs; the upper sections of short, very steep climbs; and almost any climb when you're exhausted.

Rear cogs

• Smaller — Makes it harder to turn the pedals. Used on flats and downhills.

• Larger — Makes it easier to turn the pedals. Used on climbs and most technical sections.

Terminology

"Upshift" or "shift up" means to change to a more difficult gear. "Downshift" or "shift down" means to change to an easier gear.

Gears for technical riding

Gear selection is something you really have to work out for yourself, but there are a few "rules" you need to follow.

If you forget everything else I write in this section, remember this: Anticipation is the key to shifting. In order to anticipate, you have to pay attention to the terrain changes in front of you. Sharp changes in terrain are your best signals to shift gears. Obviously, terrain changes won't magically go away just because you failed to notice them, and you can bet that other (more alert) riders will take advantage of them. Ideally, you will downshift while you still have momentum before reaching a steep uphill pitch. If you get stuck in a gear that is too high for the hill you're on, you may even have to dismount — which is frustrating because you probably could have ridden the hill if you were in the right gear.

You can clear small obstacles without shifting gears, by using momentum and carefully timed weight shifts. Henk demonstrates this technique in Figures 2.6-11. We'll discuss them later in the section "Fore-Aft Body Movement and Bunny-Hops."

When riding through an unfamiliar obstacle field, follow this rule of thumb: Pick an easy gear. On single-track it's almost always easier to spin your way out of a tight situation than it is to grind out of it in a big gear. This is particularly true when the trail gets muddy or boggy.

A few years ago, I was watching some video footage of German star Mike Kluge with some members of the British junior mountain bike team. One of the juniors marveled at Kluge as he rode across a peat bog in a World Cup race in Aviemore, Scotland: "He's so strong, but he's twiddling his pedals at about 90 (rpm). That's style!" Kluge finished on the podium in that race, no doubt assisted by his excellent gear selection.

Short, steep climbs are another common obstacle that usually require a gear change. It is a good idea to have some momentum going into this kind of climb (unless the change in terrain is so drastic that your momentum would throw you too far forward). Allow the momentum to carry you part of the way up the hill, and just before you start to slow down, shift up into an easier gear. Again, timing is everything. If you let your cadence slow too much, the shift won't work, and if you shift down too soon, you'll find yourself pedaling at something like 180 rpm. It takes practice.

As you become more proficient at shifting on short, steep climbs, start to experiment with a "double shift". This is where you simultaneously shift to the middle or inner ring in the front, and a smaller cog at the back. This allows you to maintain a more consistent pedal cadence, therefore, giving you more power and control.

Regardless of whether you are double shifting or not, you want to maintain a pedaling cadence of about 100 rpm. If you think you're about to come to a grinding halt, lean way over to one side and hop off the bike quickly, which is a much better alternative to falling off the trail sideways or tumbling backwards.

2.12-2.18 BRAKING IN DIFFICULT CONDITIONS

BRAKING

In some ways, braking is similar to shifting gears — you have to look far enough ahead to be able to react to the terrain. If you have any doubts about your brake-control skills, I recommend practicing on some gentle slopes until you've developed a sensitive touch. The kinds of things you might want to practice are gentle braking (feathering), progressively harder braking, skidding the back wheel, momentarily stopping the front wheel (be careful with this one or you'll go sailing over the bars), and pumping the brakes.

Before you do any practice runs, I strongly recommend that you make sure your brake levers are properly adjusted. The tip of the lever should travel about three-quarters of an inch before the pads contact the rim, and the lever should not be able to touch the hand grip — if it does then you will not be able to utilize your brakes fully. On the other hand, if the pads are set too close to the rim, you'll barely be able to reach the levers and have no way to modulate how much pressure the brake pads put on the rim. If you adjust the pads so that you can make a reasonable fist when applying the brakes, you should be okay.

The front and rear brakes have two very different effects. The front brake stops the bike faster, and gives you roughly 70 percent of your braking power. While the front brake is used primarily for speed reduction, the rear brake plays a more subtle role. It complements the deceleration work of the front brake, and it's also used to initiate a sideways movement of the rear wheel, which is useful in steering the bike. Even though the rear brake is less powerful than the front bike, get in the habit of using your rear brake before you apply the front brake. If you slam on the front brake, you can turn the rest of your bike into a catapult that launches you over the bars and right onto your head.

The following are examples of when to avoid using the front brake:

- very steep descents with bumps
- when turning the front wheel on a steep slope (unless you want to pivot on the front wheel)
- when the front wheel first contacts the ground after being in the air
- when the ground is very slippery or the surface is loose

In the sequence in Figures 2.12-18, Henk is on an off-camber, gravel corner that gets progressively steeper. The difficulty of this type of corner lies in preventing the front wheel from 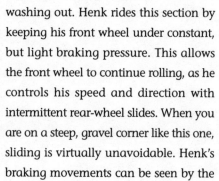 washing out. Henk rides this section by keeping his front wheel under constant, but light braking pressure. This allows the front wheel to continue rolling, as he controls his speed and direction with intermittent rear-wheel slides. When you are on a steep, gravel corner like this one, sliding is virtually unavoidable. Henk's braking movements can be seen by the puffs of dust from the rear wheel. Note that in Figure 2.18, he has passed the steepest point, at the apex of the corner. The two clouds of dust reveal that he has braked shortly before and just after the turn's apex.

When asked about this corner, Henk gave some useful pointers on braking control: "Since the most effective braking happens just before the wheel locks up, I usually try not to slide, but on tight bends, you sometimes need to get a slide going. It takes time to learn this. Like any other vehicle, it's harder to control a bike when it's sliding. So, it's useful to get the feel for how and when to do this.

"If you are still braking when you hit a corner, use the front and back brakes evenly. This way you will not place too much weight on either wheel. Sometimes you need to do a two-wheel slide around the corner. You can slide all the way through the corner without braking, by using body position alone."

As Henk says, a mountain bike does not steer as well while braking as it does when the wheels are rolling freely. Thus, when steering control is critical, you should delay the braking action — particularly on the front wheel — until the wheels are on a more stable surface or trajectory. Unless, of course, your safety is at risk.

Although locking up and skidding the back wheel can be a lot of fun, it is one of the most destructive things a mountain bike can do. Unless mountain bikers get smart about skidding their wheels, we are going to see more and more trails closed to mountain bikes. So, skid your rear wheel only as a last resort.

A common rookie mistake is using too much force in gripping the brake lever. Think of your brake levers as you would the brakes of a car: If you slam the car brakes on you can end up all over the road, but things usually go just fine with a smooth, gentle application of the brakes — even on ice.

GRIP

The pictures of Henk and Missy in this book show a great variety of grip positions. Grip is determined by the terrain and the type of shifters you have. When the going is easy, you can have a full, but relaxed, grip on the bar. If the terrain is flat and bumpy, you need to tighten your grip and let your elbows act as shock absorbers. If you need to use the brakes (when approaching an obstacle or on a descent), one or more fingers will leave the bar and rest on the levers, ready for use. It's important to send the fingers to the lever before they are needed, because this helps prevent the grabbing effect.

FORE-AFT BODY MOVEMENT AND BUNNY-HOPS

Balancing on a moving mountain bike is a complex skill, especially on uneven terrain. In order to stay balanced, you have to shift your body back and forth so your weight stays centered over the bike. Fore-aft body movements are used to help the bike flow over the terrain. With subtle weight-shifts, you can make the ride smoother and therefore less tiring and more energy-efficient. Sometimes these movements have to happen in the blink of an eye, or you'll find yourself off the trail, or face down in the dirt. Other times, it's desirable to throw your weight off-center — if for example, you want to unweight either of the wheels to make it easier to negotiate an obstacle. In extreme cases, you have to hop off the bike, and hoist it over your shoulder.

To get the feel of fore-aft movement, start by adopting Henk's position in Figure 2.4. You'll see that his knees and elbows are flexed and springy, allowing him to control the bike quickly. On your own bike, move slowly forward by placing a lot of weight on your hands, then move back so that your hips are behind the seat so you feel your weight transferred to the rear wheel. When you've gotten used to this, try lifting the front and then rear wheel from a variety of different positions to see what effect your body position has on this action.

To lift the rear wheel, flex your knees a little more than before, then do two things at once: Grip the bars firmly and rotate your wrists forward, while gently springing upward and forward on the pedals. Immediately after this, point your toes down, pushing the soles of your shoes back into the pedals and draw your feet up under you — up, back and down in one dynamic motion. It is also important to have the cranks horizontal when lifting the rear wheel.

To lift the front wheel, first drop your shoulders about six inches toward the handlebars, then rock back on the bike, sending your weight back. As your weight goes back, pull the bars toward you. If you do no more with your body movement, your front wheel will quickly fall back to the ground. But if you continue to lean back while pulling the bars back, you will do a brief wheelie before falling off backwards. (There is more on controlling a wheelie in Chapter 15.)

After practicing front and rear wheelies for a while, you will be ready to attempt a bunny-hop, demonstrated by Missy in

Figures 2.19-23. This is a skill that all mountain bikers need to master, because it's useful for clearing both small hurdles and trenches without losing speed. Execution of the bunny hop simply combines the two movements you've been practicing.

The bunny hop involves both gross and fine weight shifts that unweight different parts of the bike at specific moments. You use the gross weight shifts to bring the front and the back of the bike into the air, while the fine weight shifts keep the bike running smoothly over the ground. If riding over a small bump, you'll normally move backwards as the front wheel hits the obstacle, then forward when the back wheel hits it. This takes the weight off the wheels. In the case of larger bumps this does not apply, as Henk demonstrates in the photo sequence 2.6-11.

STEERING AND CORNERING

The basic rule of cornering a bicycle is to lean the bike, not the body. Countersteering the bike by tilting your body slightly forward and putting weight on the inside handlebar and the outside pedal, makes cornering much easier. Leaning forward puts more weight on the front wheel; leaning your outside shoulder slightly over the handlebar helps engage all the tread on your front tire. An over-exaggeration of this movement would be to twist your shoulders away from the turn.

Steering is a bit more complex, but still quite simple. Good steering technique can make a bike corner like it's on rails. Steering originates from the knees and hips, as Missy demonstrates in Figure 2.24. Her advice is "Don't steer with your hands. In most situations you're not going to turn your front wheel, you're going to lean into the turn. Use your hands more like pivot points, to transfer the energy from your elbows, and let your arms do the work. Pull up and toward your body with the outside arm and push down and away with the inside arm: the

2.19 *As Missy approaches the rocks she pushes down on the pedals, and down and forward on the handlebars. Note her bent knees and elbows.*
2.20 *At the take-off point she explodes up, getting lift principally from a powerful leg extension. Her shoulders, back and hips also rise. If you follow Missy's example, the bike will not stay on the ground.*
2.21 *To get extra wheel lift, Missy bends her knees and pulls her legs up under her.*
2.22 *A front-wheel landing is not uncommon, and riders should be prepared for it. As long as the elbows are springy and your weight is back enough, everything should work out fine.*
2.23 *The force of landing is absorbed not only by the arms, but by the legs as well. Notice how Missy's shoulders have dropped toward the handlebars. This has the beneficial side effect of weighting the front wheel to create maximum traction. From here, she recovers to the neutral position, ready for what lies ahead.*

2.24 STEERING ORIGINATES FROM THE KNEES AND HIPS.
Missy, turning to the left, points her knees and hips in the direction of the turn. In order to achieve this position, she must rotate at the waist, as if her upper body is pointing away from the direction of the turn. There are several biomechanical parallels between this and skiing. She has also articulated at the waist, leaning her upper body outward toward the vertical plane.
2.25 *Putting a foot out. This has different uses. One is to change the center of gravity; another is to help initiate a turn; yet another is to pivot around. As a last resort, it can also be used to help stay upright.*

outside arm is bent, while the inside arm is closer to being straight. Your knees and hips move into the turn, but your upper body remains square. I also put a lot of pressure on my outside pedal to exert some rotational force."

Henk agrees with Missy, "You steer with your entire body; everything makes a contribution."

When done right, steering feels relatively effortless. It's important to stay in touch with what your body is doing. This knowledge will help you focus on form, especially when the terrain makes cornering difficult. Countersteering (pulling with the outside arm and pushing with the inside arm, while putting weight on the outside pedal and turning with your knees and hips) may sound backwards and confusing. All I can tell you is to try it. I find that I can go through a turn about 5 mph faster when I am using good countersteering techniques.

If you want to get around a tight corner at low speeds, make a conscious effort to turn the handlebars as you tilt the bike into the turn, and then lean out against the turn. At medium and high speeds, forget about turning the bars — that will take care of itself.

If all this leaning without turning the handlebars has gotten you a little confused, try walking beside your bike while holding onto the saddle. When the bike is upright, it travels in a straight line. Lean the bike toward you, and the front wheel turns and

the rear wheel follows, although in a tighter arc. Lean the bike away from you, and the same thing happens in the opposite direction. So you see that turning the handlebars is not required to make a turn.

In Figure 2.25, Missy demonstrates another basic cornering technique: putting the inside foot out, which allows her to take steep, gravely turns with more speed. This technique is seldom practiced by cross-country riders, because the seat is normally too high to make this technique useful. Dangling a foot does, however, give away some control, because you then lose the close relationship between inner thigh and seat, and you temporarily lose the option of pushing against one of your pedals. Control is further reduced by hitting bumps when dangling a leg; although, the speed gained in the corners more than compensates for the momentary lack of control — unless, of course, you crash.

BASIC JUMP

Both cross-country and downhill riders need to know how to jump a bike. Jumping is an excellent way to avoid certain obstacles, and no matter how good of a rider you are, sooner or later you're going to get airborne, so you better know how to land.

The two main difficulties riders get into when jumping are not staying upright, and doing an endo upon landing. The first problem happens when a rider approaches the jump off balance or pulls up too sharply on one side of the handlebars. Both of these problems create rotational forces that get worse as the bike travels through the air. By that time it's too late, and all the rider can hope for is a good recovery on the landing.

To avoid problems in midair, practice on a jump that has an easy run-up and a smooth landing surface. As you approach the jump, your shoulders and hips should be square with the lip of the jump. At take-off, don't pull up on the handlebars, but spring up with your legs, as if for a small bunny hop. Let your upper body remain calm, and start moving slightly back as you spring. Practice, practice, practice.

This brings us to the second part: the landing. Always select a practice jump with a landing area that slopes downhill. This reduces your chance of doing an endo.

As I mentioned before, move your weight up and back at the take-off, and continue moving back until you are fractionally behind the center of your saddle. Pull up and back, with your legs while down and back on the pedals with your toes pointing down. If you tie all this together, the jump should be easy. When you land, absorb the shock by bending your knees and elbows.

If your weight is centered too far forward and an endo looks imminent, it might be best to bail out and curl up into a ball, thus reducing the risk of a broken collarbone. If you think you have any chance of pulling the jump off, stay centered and get back as far as you can and hope for the best. Whatever you do, don't touch the brakes until you're rolling safely away from the landing area.

In Figures 2.26-28, Missy gives a textbook demonstration of a basic jump, which is all you need to know for starters.

MENTAL MAPS

Picking a line and sticking to it can be difficult, especially on single-track. Visualizing your path down the trail can be helpful. Try stopping at the beginning of the section, picking out the line you want to take, and building a mental map of the entire section. Imagine yourself progressing along this line, seeing everything from your rider's-eye view. Then ride it. Just keep looking at the line you want to take, and let your bike follow your eyes. Don't look at where you don't want to go, because as soon as you look there, that's where you'll go. If you get off line, don't worry about it. Just keep looking ahead and find another line. You'll be surprised how fast another one shows up.

SUMMARY

The basics of position and control may take years to master, especially if you haven't been riding all your life. Even if this stuff seems hard at first, all these skills can become part of your repertoire with regular practice. My advice is to hang in there, keep practicing, and take it one step at a time. Remember, there are no medals given out for bravery; so don't attempt anything that feels way over your head.

Like Henk says, "Don't do anything stupid. Lots of times people get hurt trying to imitate their better-skilled friends. If you have doubts about riding something, you're not going to ride it successfully. To learn new things, always take an easy option ... and progress little by little."

The goal of all these skills is to fine-tune your riding, which allows you to have more fun — which is the reason you started riding a mountain bike in the first place. Improved riding skills also allow you to get from A to B using less energy. Another way to make more efficient use of your energy is by fitness training. Mountain bike training is a mixed bag of exercises, some of which are explained in the next chapter on the essentials of physiology and the principles of fitness and training.

2.26 *At take-off, Missy allows her front wheel to climb into the air and springs with her legs. Any pull on the handlebars must be even between the two hands.*
2.27 *Moving through the air, she remains poised and positioned slightly behind the center.*
2.28 *On landing, she flexes her elbows and knees as she absorbs the shock.*

Chapter 3

The physiology of training

THE HEART OF THE MATTER
Being specific

Training is primarily about specificity. To respond to the demands placed on your body during a mountain bike race, you have to train your muscles and energy systems. All cross training aside, the only way to prepare for mountain bike racing is by training on a bike, doing very specific exercises that imitate the stresses of a mountain bike race.

Please don't misconstrue this advice by going out and riding your mountain bike every day as if you were racing. That would kill you. You have to factor in some easy rides as well as hard ones, and you'll also have to train on the road in order to reach your full potential. Yes, the road: that black asphalt stuff with all the cars on it. Forget about that roadie versus mountain bike rivalry — that went out with toe-clips. If you want the best high-intensity endurance training that two wheels, a chain, some pedals and a frame can offer, nothing is better than a good, stiff dose of road riding. This is because it is easier to maintain a steady heart rate for an entire training period on the road. You also don't have to recover from the physical beating that race-pace off-road training can dish out.

Now, don't panic — off-road riding unquestionably plays a major role in your training plan. But to use your off-road training effectively, you need to supplement it with smart, scientifically proven techniques, which include road riding. Obviously, mountain bike riding skills can only be practiced in the dirt, so you'll need to devote a significant amount of your training time to them. Besides, it's important to tear it up a little bit and have a good time, because feeling free and loose on your bike is a key component to your motivation. If you don't feel good about your training, then chances are you won't do it. In general terms, think about the road for beefing-up and fine-tuning your engine, and think about the dirt for base training and bike-handling techniques.

What about cross training?

Specificity in cross training is slightly more complicated. Cross training is good because it can provide a means of conditioning when you don't feel like riding. You may find that after a couple of weeks of cross training at the end of the year, you're ready to come back to mountain biking with a renewed zest. And even though cross training sports like basketball, ice hockey, tennis, soccer, cross-country skiing, running and mountaineering take away from your mountain bike performance, the trade-off in terms of enthusiasm more than makes up for it.

While we're on the topic, don't confuse cross training with supplementary exercises. Supplementary exercises are designed to give you extra strength and agility and can be performed year round. Weight training is one of the most common types of supplementary exercises. When it comes to weight training, be careful to select the best exercises for the development of your cycling muscles (for example, bench presses and lat pull downs are good for overall conditioning — but do very little to improve your leg strength). Additionally, lifting heavy weights may be good for increasing your muscle-fiber recruitment potential, but it's only useful if the muscles are actually needed for cycling — the muscles of the legs, butt and lower back.

Specificity in muscle conditioning for downhill racing dictates that exercises should be aimed at giving good performance over a period ranging between four and six minutes.

There will be more on weight training later in the book.

BART BRENTJENS: A CASE STUDY

Dutch rider Bart Brentjens won the Grundig World Cup cross-country title in 1994, but by the middle of the '95 season he was experiencing the worst performances of his professional career. As a result, he sought the advice of his brother-in-law, the recently-retired road professional, Gert-Jan Theunisse. Together they concluded that an excess of high-intensity off-road training was gradually wearing Brentjens down.

So Brentjens switched his hard training rides from dirt to motorpaced road work. The effects of this transition were epic. In the second half of the 1995 season, Brentjens won the mountain bike Tour de France (Le Tour VTT), finished second in the final two World Cup races and went on to win the world cross-country championship.

Brentjens says that he's convinced that too many hard off-road training miles rendered him uncompetitive. This view is supported by several other leading pro riders, including two-time cross-country world champion Alison Sydor and multi-U.S. champion Ned Overend. Another advocate of road work for mountain bike racers is British pro mountain bike racer Gary Foord, a part-time trainer of sport-class riders. Foord advocates road riding for the majority of race-pace sessions, supplemented by off-road work for long moderate-pace rides and the occasional shorter, high-intensity workout.

PHYSIOLOGY

Specificity in training comes under two main headings: biomechanics and physiology. Specificity in biomechanics means you must practice limb movements exactly as you would make them in a mountain bike race. Specificity in physiology requires that you choose appropriate training for the different energy systems that provide fuel for the biomechanical movements. We'll work with physiology in this chapter, while the later "skills" chapters will focus on biomechanics.

An awareness of the most important aspects of energy pro-

duction will help make it clearer to you why you need to vary the intensity, frequency and duration of your training sessions.

Lactate threshold: A reference point

Your energy-production systems can be divided into two broad categories: aerobic and anaerobic. Aerobic means "with oxygen"; anaerobic means "without oxygen". This distinction will mean more to you as we delve further into this chapter.

The term and concept of lactate threshold (LT) is controversial in exercise-physiology circles. The words suggest that on one side of the threshold we do not produce lactic acid, and that on the other side we do. In practice, this does not happen because both anaerobic and aerobic energy sources are almost always in operation. What does happen is an internal shift in demand from aerobic energy sources to anaerobic energy sources. This shift occurs near the lactate threshold, and it all happens in response to your decision to move your legs faster and faster.

In order to describe this process more accurately, the lactate threshold has been given many names, including deflection point, anaerobic threshold, and onset of blood lactate accumulation (OBLA). But while some scientists continue in their efforts to pinpoint exactly what is happening at lactate threshold, no one really disagrees about its importance as a general concept.

For an endurance athlete, the concept of lactate threshold provides an important reference point for determining relative

When It Starts to Hurt

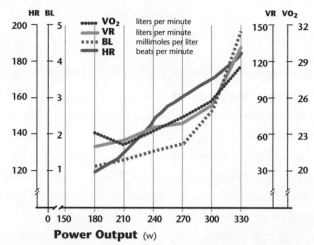

VO₂ amount of air breathed in to get 1 liter of air to the working muscles

DIAGRAM 3.1

We can see that around 300w, ventilation and blood lactate rise steeply, although heart rate is relatively linear. It is highly likely that the rider's threshold is in this area.

levels of training intensity — that is, levels above and below your threshold.

So, how do you recognize your lactate threshold? First, it is important that you become familiar with your measurable body signs as lactate threshold is reached and passed.

Imagine you are out on your bike, riding up a steady climb and increasing your speed as you go. As your exercise intensity increases, you can feel your heart rate and breathing frequency also increase. This is illustrated in Diagram 3.1. As you keep going faster, your heart is pounding in your chest, and you have to concentrate on your breathing. You notice that speech is becoming increasingly difficult, and limited to one or two monosyllabic words at a time. If you continue to push harder, your breathing will become faster and more difficult to control. Once speech is no longer an option, you have gone over your threshold, and soon you'll have to slow down.

VO2 MAX OR HEART-RATE MAX?

VO_2 max is also known as maximum oxygen uptake. The "V" stands for volume, and of course, O_2 is for oxygen. This figure represents the maximum amount of oxygen you can breathe in and transport to your muscles and organs for energy production. This means that your VO_2 max is reached at a very high intensity of exercise. VO_2 max is normally measured in metric liters per minute. This measurement can be either an absolute figure, like 4.5 l/min, or it can be relative to your body weight in kilograms (one kilogram equals 2.2046 pounds), where it is given as milliliters per kilogram body weight, per minute, as in 68 ml/kg min.

As an adult, maximum oxygen uptake doesn't change greatly after you have two or three years of serious training under your belt. Junior racers, however, can expect big changes associated with growth and maturation. For instance, as your lungs get larger, you should be able to take in more O_2.

VO_2 max is not your exercise-intensity ceiling. You can work above it, and your heart rate will still continue to rise to its maximum and your power output will still increase, but these increases are accounted for by the anaerobic metabolism — that system of energy production which is not dependent on oxygen. For mountain bikers, exercise above the VO_2 max intensity cannot be sustained for much more than a minute. The object of endurance training is to produce more power across your VO_2 range.

Statistically speaking, VO_2 max is a good predictor of performance. Athletes with a very high VO_2 max stand a better chance of reaching the top ranks of competition; however, don't let that discourage you if you have a low VO_2 max value. Athletes with values close to 70 ml/kg min have also been successful racers — especially in downhill, where efficient movement and bike handling skills are so important.

A good analogy can be made between VO_2 max and a car's engine capacity. The bigger the engine, the more power it can produce. But if the car is heavily laden, or the engine isn't working right, the car won't necessarily go faster than a more efficient vehicle with a smaller engine.

A mountain bike rider with a high VO_2 max has the potential for very high aerobic power. But can he or she make his or her energy production and delivery systems efficient enough to utilize all of it? If not, that racer might be beaten by a more efficient rider with a lower VO_2 max. You see, VO_2 max is only one in a very long list of factors that goes into the making of a mountain bike racer. My suggestion is not to focus on it.

VO_2 Max vs. heart rate max

Should you use VO_2 max or heart rate max to calculate your training heart rates? For simplicity's sake, heart rate max is the figure most commonly used. Also, VO_2 max heart rate doesn't change much in relation to heart rate max if you're training regularly.

Lactate Threshold: A Moveable Point

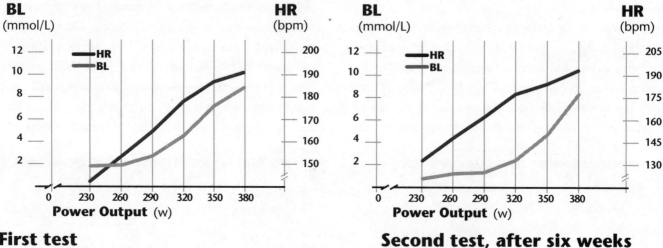

First test

Second test, after six weeks hard training

Data taken from elite-level male mountain-bike racer in pre-season training

DIAGRAM 3.2
Data for this graph was taken from a test on an 18-year-old male elite-level mountain biker. His hr max was 206 bpm; VO$_2$ max: 72.6 ml/kg/min; max power output: 417w.

Note: We can see at around 300w blood lactate rises steeply, although heart rate is relatively linear. It is highly likely that the rider's threshold is in this area.

Why? Besides not being able to get enough air, the main thing that causes you to slow down is the concentration of lactic acid in your muscles and blood. Looking at a lactate line (the concentration of lactic acid in your blood or muscles) on the graph, you can see that the slope of the line rises steadily until a certain point, where the slope suddenly becomes much steeper. The point on the graph where the slope of the line suddenly changes coincides with your lactate threshold. Not surprisingly, this is why it's called the lactate threshold. Below the lactate threshold, your body is working aerobically; once you move above the lactate threshold, the body can no longer keep up with the rapid accumulation of lactic acid in the muscles. This is called anaerobic metabolism.

It's important for you to know that your lactate threshold is dynamic, rather than fixed, and responds to your physiological status. The way we plot its movement is by measuring heart rate. Sports scientists have identified strong correlation between heart rate, blood-lactate concentration, work rate, and oxygen consumption. These correlations have turned out to be invaluable in providing training signposts for endurance athletes. The point of all this is that you can increase your lactate threshold level — that is, the percentage of VO$_2$ max at which you reach your threshold.

NOTES OF CAUTION

① Periodically monitor your lactate threshold heart rate — every eight to 12 weeks is good. Your threshold moves around in response to the type of training you do; by keeping note of it, you can be sure of keeping your training on track.
② Don't be fooled by a reduced heart rate. A low heart rate is the sign of a well-trained cyclist, but it is also the sign of an overtrained cyclist. If your heart rate is lower than normal, but you don't feel great and have difficulty getting your heart rate as high as you normally can, take a break from training. You might need a week off the bike — you might need a month or more. Sudden death from symptoms associated with Athletic Heart Syndrome are not uncommon, so I strongly recommend that you consult a physician immediately if you are experiencing the following symptoms: sudden light-headedness, heart palpitations or chest pain.

The relationship between lactate threshold and VO_2 max is important. The better your condition, the closer your threshold will be to your VO_2 max. And, as you now know, this relationship is prone to change. The same can be said for lactate threshold and heart rate. As a rule, the better your condition, the higher your heart rate is at lactate threshold. Therefore, you must periodically monitor your threshold and, if necessary, adjust your training heart rate, to progressively increase your performance, or to avert overtraining.

In practice, all of the different intensities of training you do are calculated in relation to your lactate threshold.

Training by feel

Some athletes prefer to disregard heart rate and gauge intensity by how they feel. This approach has produced some of our greatest athletes, so it can't be ignored. For some, the rapid feedback of a heart rate monitor is not at all welcome. For others, stopping to manually record heart rate can be disruptive to a training session. Still others simply can't justify the expense of a heart rate monitor. If you fall into any of these categories, take note of the section on feelings of intensity, detailed in appendix two.

Among very experienced riders, feel is fairly reliable. But it has many pitfalls for the less experienced. Factors such as dietary status and residual fatigue can both confound the way you feel, as can your mood. Unless it's malfunctioning, your heart rate monitor doesn't lie. If you examine its feedback alongside information from your training diary, you should be able to make a fairly accurate assessment of your physical state.

Training mix and energy production

Lactate threshold works as a reference point for relative training intensity, but we should also look at the broader concept of training mix. Training mix is a standard, widely recognized set of training principles. It covers the three main variables that affect your entire training year: intensity, duration and frequency. At any time in the year, you should have a clear idea of how hard (intensity), how long (duration), and how often (frequency) you should be training. This way you can tailor your exercise program to suit your individual needs.

Working out an effective training program isn't difficult when you start to look at it in terms of apportioning your effort into training all of the different energy systems. As you come to understand how your body produces the energy you use to train and race, you will gain clearer insight into how and why you should split up your training.

HOW EFFICIENT IS YOUR ENGINE?

Humans are, unfortunately not very efficient at energy conversion. It's rather frustrating to know that only about 20 percent of the energy we produce goes toward fueling muscle movement. The remaining 80 percent is converted into heat production.

THE ENERGY SYSTEMS

The production of energy for muscle movement is an involved and complex subject. In simplified and relevant terms it goes something like the following. Fuel for muscle movement comes from several different sources. What they all have in common is the end product, a substance called adenosine triphosphate, or ATP. ATP energizes the microscopic back-and-forth sliding action of filaments inside the millions of cells making up a muscle. This sliding enables the muscle to extend or contract. ATP is always available to muscles, because without it the filaments do not slide and rigor occurs — in which case the body becomes stiff like a dead animal. The prevention of rigor is one reason why several systems are available to ensure that the muscle always has a ready supply of ATP.

In light exercise, relatively little ATP is required; in strenuous exercise, a lot of ATP is required. But muscle cells store only enough for one to two seconds' worth of strenuous exercise.

Anaerobic systems produce ATP by simple, and therefore more rapid processes than the aerobic system. Anaerobic systems, however, either have relatively small reserves, or as a byproduct produce chemicals that can cause muscle dysfunction. We call on anaerobic systems when we need a lot of energy quickly, for instance when charging to make it up a short, steep incline, or simply when rising from a chair. In contrast, aerobic systems don't work quickly enough to supply the energy for these purposes, but they are relatively inexhaustible.

PCr system

The fastest ATP production process is the creatine phosphate or PCr, system. ATP stores are quickly replenished by the substance creatine phosphate (PCr). The PCr system fuels short bursts of energy, and is used by mountain bikers at the starting-line sprint, and then again on very short, steep pitches and during brief sprinting efforts. The main limit of the PCr system is that the "phosphate battery", as it is also known, is very

PCr + ADP ———> creatine + ATP

When ATP releases energy for muscle movement, it's converted to ADP. To reconvert that ADP back to ATP, a PCr molecule gives up a phosphate group, along with energy, to the ADP to form ATP, and creatine is left over. This creatine then accepts the phosphate group back when the process is reversed, which happens as ATP demand slows down. PCr stores can then build up again.

DIAGRAM 3.3 DIAGRAMMING THE PCR SYSTEM

quickly emptied. Depending on the intensity of exercise, this may be somewhere between five and 10 seconds. With much hard work, the PCr system can be trained to turn out a little more ATP, but then it's only a few extra seconds' worth.

Creatine phosphate may be rapidly depleted, but it's also rapidly replenished during rest and relatively low-intensity exercise. After just 20 seconds of rest, about half of it has been replaced, and after 45 seconds, stocks are back to about three-quarters full. The remainder takes a matter of minutes.

In sprint training sessions, the delay between sprints is intended to allow the PCr supplies to refill and lactic acid to diffuse. For purposes of fully replenished muscles, then, rest periods in sprint training shouldn't be less than two to five minutes.

Glycolysis, or the lactic acid system

The other anaerobic system has two common names: glycolysis and the lactic acid system. The terms glycolytic and glycolysis refer to the breakdown of glycogen, the body's stored form of glucose.

The chain looks like this:

Entry through the mouth (ingestion) -> digestion -> absorption -> blood glucose -> muscle and liver glycogen

DIAGRAM 3.4

Most of the body's glycogen is stored in muscle and in the liver. The metabolism of glycogen is shown in Diagram 3.6. Glycogen is converted to glucose in the muscle when it's needed for energy.

Glucose + 2ATP ———> 4ATP + Pyruvic Acid

DIAGRAM 3.5

This is another anaerobic process, taking place without oxygen, inside the muscle. The burning of glucose yields a net gain of two units of ATP, but it also produces a byproduct called pyruvic acid. In the absence of oxygen, pyruvic acid is con-verted to lactic acid. At low-intensity exercise, when oxygen is abundant, pyruvic acid is removed and converted in a longer process to form more ATP. At high-intensity exercise — namely the lactate threshold — your aerobic system is consuming all available oxygen, and so if you want to go still faster, you do so at the cost of a lactic acid build-up.

The lactic acid produced in glycolysis is carried in the blood to the liver, where, if sufficient oxygen becomes available (in light exercise for example), it's converted to glucose. This glucose may then return to the muscle. At exercise intensities above the lactate threshold, sufficient oxygen isn't available to convert the lactic acid and glucose. This is why, if you spend too long above your threshold level, a build-up of lactic acid occurs. If the exercise intensity is not decreased to below the threshold level within a minute or two, the lactic acid starts to cause several short-term problems, of which muscular pain is the most pronounced. This pain is associated with muscle dysfunction, as the lactic acid inhibits the mechanisms that make the muscle contract. At this time, choice goes out the window, and you're forced to slow down.

Oxidative metabolism

No one system operates in isolation to provide ATP for muscle contraction. When the aerobic system becomes overloaded, anaerobic providers — mainly the lactic acid system — are called upon. One of the tenets of training, however, is to condition the body to provide as much energy as possible through the aerobic system.

The aerobic system is fueled by carbohydrates, fats and protein. We can overlook protein as an energy source, because its metabolism to ATP is very complex and slow. Protein is a principal energy provider only in extreme situations, such as ultra-distance events or starvation. But protein does play a leading role in other functions, such as the formation and repair of body tissue.

Carbohydrates are converted to glucose or glycogen and metabolized with oxygen. If this process is diagrammed, it looks like this:

**glucose + oxygen + ADP ——> ATP
+ water + carbon dioxide**

DIAGRAM 3.6

Fats are converted to free fatty acids and metabolized with oxygen.

This is diagrammed like this:

Fat + oxygen + ADP ——> ATP + water + carbon dioxide

DIAGRAM 3.7

Most byproducts of energy metabolism are dumped into the blood for reprocessing or excretion. Carbon dioxide, for example, passes out of the body through the lungs.

Aerobic systems normally start making a significant contribution to energy production after about two minutes of exercise. They may be slow to fire up, but they can keep us going for hours, even days on end. For mountain bikers, energy from fat is almost unlimited, but the energy stored in carbohydrate (glycogen) form amounts to about 2000 kilo-calories of energy in a full-grown adult. This amount of energy can fuel up to two hours of heavy exercise.

In practice, fat and carbohydrates share the burden of the body's energy demand. They each have different strengths. The metabolism of fat requires more oxygen than does the metabolism of carbohydrates, and the conversion of fats to glycogen is slower. But fat stores remain plentiful long after carbohydrates have been depleted. When riders talk about "blowing up," "hitting the wall" or "bonking," they're referring to hav-

ENERGY PRODUCTION AND RPMS

ATP is required in greater or lesser quantities, depending on the speed or force of muscle contraction. In a rapidly repeated movement, such as pedaling at 180 rpm, a relatively light force might be exerted with each pedal stroke, but over the course of one minute a relatively small number of fibers have contracted a great number of times — therefore, the ATP demand is high. In a different situation, turning a big gear at 80 rpm can also stimulate a high ATP demand because a greater number of fibers are recruited in the working muscles, even though the speed of the contraction is lower. Partly for this reason, it's good to train at both high and low revs — just as you will inevitably find yourself riding in different parts of a race.

OVERLOAD: THE ROAD TO IMPROVEMENT

I've already suggested that training adaptation comes in response to overloading the system. Although it's necessary to improve physical performance, overload isn't really all that good for the body (which is one reason why hard training hurts). Without overload, there's no need for any adaptation, and no improvement in condition will occur. Be careful about how you factor overloading into your training. The rest of this book should help you find the appropriate way to do this.

ing severely depleted their carbohydrate stores (alternatively, they could mean they've spent too much time over the lactate threshold and are forced to slow down for a while). You may have experienced carbohydrate depletion yourself: You would have been able to continue riding, but at a very slow pace. And you probably would have felt ravenously hungry. This state feels a little uncomfortable, often because of the bile sloshing about in your stomach. A light-headed feeling is also common in carbohydrate depletion. Riders go so slowly when they hit the wall because their work rate is limited by the speed at which ATP can be produced by fat.

At rest, fat contributes the greatest proportion of fuel, but as exercise intensity increases to a moderate level the proportion of fats and carbohydrates becomes approximately equal. In heavy exercise, where anaerobic processes are involved, carbohydrates contribute a greater proportion of the fuel than fat does.

Diets very high in carbohydrate have been shown to be far more effective than high-fat diets for fueling high-intensity endurance exercise. However, take note that, in their seminal work, *Textbook of Work Physiology*, Strand and Rodahl advised athletes competing in one- to two-hour endurance events against regularly consuming a diet high in carbohydrates, since this would condition the body to increase its dependence on carbohydrates, rather than fat, as a fuel.

In this book, you'll learn that one of the main aims in endurance training is to increase the body's capacity to burn fats as fuel during the first hour of a race, thus sparing more carbohydrates for combustion later in the event.

So although the emphasis should be on carbohydrates, don't

forget that fat metabolism remains a fundamental source of energy for your effort. And don't forget that dietary fat is essential to metabolize carbohydrates and protein.

TRAINING THEORY

Now let's move on to training theory. To begin, we'll return to the three fundamental variables, all of which must be frequently adjusted. Again, these are: intensity, duration and frequency.

Intensity

The key word in improving athletic condition is overload. Improvements to your condition will only come if you overload your energy systems. If this overload is repeated, the body makes physiological changes so that what once was an overload is an overload no more. This adaptation is known as the training effect.

The two main questions here are, which system should you overload, and by how much?

Your training intensity level determines which energy system you're placing the most load on. For purposes of training analysis, it's far simpler if you focus on only one system per session. Mountain bike racers should train to overload each of their energy systems. By correctly matching your training intensity level to the energy system you want to train, you can ensure that your training covers all the normal physiological demands of a mountain bike race. How to do this is explained in Chapters 4 through 9.

Duration

Duration is closely linked to intensity. No one can sprint for

PROGRESSION

When the body has adapted to a specific training load, it can no longer be considered an overload. Continued and progressive improvement in conditioning will only come through successive increases in the intensity and duration of sessions. Progress should be made in gradual increments, in respect of the slow speed at which physiological changes take place. Too rapid a progression inevitably leads to that most debilitating and confusing of physical conditions: overtraining.

10 minutes, and a sprint-length session performed at endurance intensity would be worthless. So duration is all about deciding on the optimum length of time for performing a training exercise at a given intensity. At the highest levels of intensity, adjustment in duration can be sensitive to just a couple of seconds.

Apart from intensity, other factors used to determine the duration of a session are:

• Physical condition
• Nutritional status
• Training period in the year
• Atmospheric conditions such as daylight, humidity and temperature

After reading later chapters, you'll be more familiar with how these concepts affect duration.

Frequency

How often you train is known as frequency. So if a coach asked you what was the frequency of your aerobic power training sessions, you might reply, "Twice a week during period three." (Periodization of training will be explained in Chapter 7.)

One of the biggest factors to consider when determining your training frequency is "rest." Rest is very valuable because it is the time when you allow for muscular recovery after training. These rest periods provide for physiological adaptation, which will reduce the stress impact of the last overload session. It's important to note that improvements in condition actually take place during rest periods, not exercise periods. However, to make the fastest improvements in condition, the next overload training session (as opposed to recovery session) should take place at the earliest possible time. Intake of extra water and carbohydrates during and immediately after exercise will help to reduce the necessary recovery time.

Putting the variables together

Combining the three variables of intensity, frequency and duration will determine what kind of condition you're in. By changing the ratios you can alter your training program to find optimal condition for anything from the kilometer sprint on the velodrome in Atlanta, to the multi-day Sydney-Perth mountain bike race on the red dust of Australia's outback.

Careful manipulation of a structured training program also alters your state of condition during the year, allowing you to produce your best performances during a chosen period. However, in order to accomplish this, a certain protocol of periodization must be followed. Periodization will be explained in Chapter 7. For the moment, let me give the example that short-

REVERSIBILITY

Peak fitness is hard to gain but easy to lose. If a period of illness or injury prevents training for even a few days, it's important to resume training at a lower level than where you dropped off. In this way training programs must be flexible.

er, harder sessions may increase your speed, but have maximum effect for you as a mountain bike racer only if they're performed as an over-layer, on top of a good endurance base.

SUMMARY

In summary, I'd like to remind you of four important points.

❶ Training must be specific.

❷ The lactate threshold concept provides an important reference point for training. The majority of fitness training for mountain biking is performed at an intensity just under this threshold level.

❸ Our bodies rely on different systems to produce the ATP that fuels muscle contraction. These systems are the PCr, anaerobic glycolysis, and aerobic systems. Each system comes into play during a mountain bike race, although we should strive to stress the glycolytic system as little as possible during a race, because stressing it has been shown to reduce performance late in the race.

❹ A successful training program alters the ratios of intensity, duration and frequency of exercise according to the time of year and the goals of the rider.

The next chapter is an introduction to training programs, and then Chapter 5 will outline some of the ways used to measure and monitor lactate threshold, so it can be used as a training guide.

Chapter 4

Introduction to training programs

Now that you understand the basics of training physiology, you're probably wondering how to apply this information to your own workouts. The training sessions outlined in this chapter will help — you'll be glad to know that these sessions can be tailored to your individual needs and then slotted into the training programs outlined in Chapters 7 and 9.

Keep in mind that while the individual training sessions in this book are easy enough, the problems begin when sessions are strung together to form an overall training plan. All too many times, training programs are too hard and time-consuming. Your training schedule has to be flexible, allowing you to adjust it as you progress, or to reschedule sessions to accommodate other events in your life. This advice applies to all riders who have a life, so I assume this means you.

I've outlined the different types of training sessions, but before you read about them, please note a few things that will make these sessions much easier to understand and more efficient to do:

① The first point is to develop a high tolerance for abbreviations; a number of them are used in this and following chapters.
② I always recommend 10 to 15 minutes of stretching before exercise, and then warming up for 10 to 20 minutes. In addition, I recommend cooling down for 10 to 30 minutes, and then finishing with 10 to 15 minutes of stretching. I know that a lot of you don't have the inclination to do this, and I can't reach out of these pages and force you. It's up to you. You might note there is no need for a warm up before a recovery ride, but if you go into a high-intensity session without warming up, you will waste the first 15 minutes of the session, and quite possibly damage a muscle or tendon.
③ Suggestions for duration are tailored for accomplished riders in the sport category and upwards. Junior, women and novice riders are given separate suggestions.
④ In talking about training heart rates, I favor the heart-rate reserve method of calculation (see the following sidebar on heart-

CALCULATING HEART-RATE RESERVE

Please note that in order to translate the following equations, you'll want to use the following key: mhr = maximum heart rate; rhr = resting heart rate; p = the percentage you choose; thr = training heart rate. All heart-rate figures are to be given in beats per minute, or bpm.

To work out the heart-rate reserve:

$$mhr - rhr = \text{heart-rate reserve}$$

To figure out a training heart rate:

$$(\text{heart-rate reserve}) \times p + rhr = thr$$

Here's an example for a rider with a 197 bpm maximum heart rate and a 48 bpm resting heart rate.

To figure out the heart rate reserve:

$$197 - 48 = 149$$

Now, if that person wants to exercise at 80 percent, then he or she applies the following equation:

$$(149 \times 0.8) + 48 = 119 + 48 = 167$$

You might note that calculating this as 80 percent of your maximum heart rate would only have given 158 bpm.

Session Code	Intensity (given as percentage of heart rate reserve)	Duration of each Repetition	Number of Repetitions	Active Recovery	Mode (0n- or off-road)	Type: (Interval, repeat or steady state)	System stressed
PCr	maximum	10 seconds	10-15	2-3 min between reps 5-6 min between sets	off-road	repetitions	anaerobic: phosphate battery
LT	90% +	1-2 min	4-10	40 sec-1 min	on- or off-road	intervals or reps	anaerobic: glycogen
AP	80-90% (2)	4-6 min	Up to 6x6 min Up to 9x4 min	3-4 min between reps (1)	on- or off-road	intervals or reps	aerobic: glycogen/fat
HIE	75-80%	15-60 + min	Optional: 1x60; 2x30; 3x20; 4x15.	5 min if you break session up into reps	on-road	steady state	aerobic: glycogen/fat
LIE	60-75%	1-3 hours	Not less than 1 hour blocks	none	on- or off-road	steady state	aerobic: fat/glycogen
REC	less than 60%	30 min-2 hours	none	none	on- or off-road	steady state	aerobic: fat/glycogen

TABLE 4.1 THE RANGE OF TRAINING SESSIONS

Notes:

① *Find the 50-percent rate by using the heart-rate reserve calculation (deduct rhr from mhr). Multiply the result by 0.5, then add back your rhr figure.*

② *If your heart rate has not dropped to the 50-percent rate within five minutes after exercise, it might be because of one of the following: You are riding too intensively; a little over-trained; or simply beat, and it's time to cruise home.*

③ *An accomplished elite-class rider may be able to ride at 90-percent without producing unacceptably high lactate levels. Most riders, however, will be closer to the 80-percent level. If in doubt, underestimate — it's far easier to*

correct mistakes then.

④ *I've included a range of times and intensities to cater to as wide a group of readers as possible. In reality, there will be some overlap. For example, while 85-percent of the heart-rate range might be an aerobic intensity for one rider, it might be anaerobic for another. If you have any uncertainty about how much time to give each repetition, or which end of the intensity range, opt for less time and lower intensity — that way you have a reduced risk of overtraining.*

rate reserve for an explanation of this opinion).

⑤ If you are over 30 years old, or new to endurance exercise, and do not have an idea of your maximum heart rate, there is a cautious approach to defining your mhr. Simply deduct your age from 220. This figure is merely a rough guess, but should be close enough to suffice for six months or so, by which time you should be able to undergo a mhr test without any great risk to your heart.

Tips

Active recovery — Keep pedaling, in a really easy gear, during active recovery periods. Aim for a heart rate of 50 percent heart-rate reserve.

THE SESSIONS EXPLAINED
Recovery (REC)

Recovery rides are beneficial because they increase blood flow through the muscles, bringing rich supplies of oxygen and nutrients, and speeding the removal of the by-products of high-intensity exercise.

Recovery rides as discussed here should follow a race or hard training. Some of the more experienced racers like to take a 30-minute recovery spin on the day of the race, although many

are content to wait until the next day.

If you want to practice some skills on a recovery ride, there should be no problem with that, as long as you do not exercise above 60-percent of heart-rate reserve.

The recovery ride can also be a social session, and it can be as long as the group is content to ride at the pace of the slowest member.

RECOVERY

INTENSITY: less than 60-percent heart-rate reserve

DURATION: 30 minutes to 2 hours

FREQUENCY: up to three days a week

TERRAIN: on or off-road, flat or gentle undulations

TYPE/MAIN FUEL: aerobic/fat

CADENCE: 80-100 rpm

JUNIORS: 1-2 hours; WOMEN: 1-2 hours; NOVICES: 30 minutes to 1 hour

Low Intensity Endurance (LIE)

This is the way to lay the foundations of an endurance base, to get into the swing of pedaling for more than an hour at a time, and to train your body to burn fat as fuel. The more efficient your body becomes at burning fat, the more "higher octane" glycogen is spared for when you need it at increased intensities. LIE riding starts about one month after your last race of the season and continues as your staple training ride for eight weeks. The duration of a LIE ride begins with one hour for beginners, and goes up to three hours for pros and serious amateurs. If you really want to, you can do more — but I wouldn't recommend it.

If you want to mix skills practice sessions in with one of these rides, fine by me, but if you do, make sure to do at least one hour of uninterrupted LIE riding.

On a LIE ride, your heart rate shouldn't rise above 75-percent of its maximum. This means that if you encounter hills you might need to make a special effort to go slowly and make your gear selection accordingly. On the descents, it might be necessary to work harder than usual to keep your pulse up around the 65- to 70-percent mark, but it's not worth risking a crash to do this.

Some coaches recommend taking only water on these rides; others believe that sipping a carbohydrate solution every 15 minutes helps your blood-sugar content level, while you still metabolize fats. And make doubly sure that you start out at least two hours following a meal (as you should with all training sessions). This will ensure that your body works on burning fat.

LOW INTENSITY ENDURANCE

INTENSITY: 65- to 75-percent heart-rate reserve
DURATION: 1-3 hours
FREQUENCY: up to five times a week
TERRAIN: on or off-road, flat or gentle undulations
TYPE/MAIN FUEL: aerobic/fat
CADENCE: 80-100 rpm
JUNIORS: 2-3 hours; WOMEN: 1-3 hours; NOVICES: 1-2 hours

LIE: If MAX PR=180 LT=170

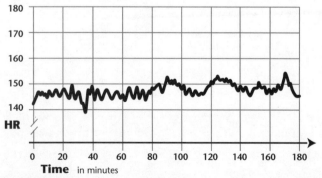

DIAGRAM 4.3 LOW INTENSITY ENDURANCE

WHY YOU SHOULD BASE CALCULATIONS ON HEART-RATE RESERVE

Heart-rate reserve is an important concept because it relates to the heart-rate range used over and above that needed by the resting body. Using the simple maximum heart-rate percentage calculation does not account for training- or health-induced changes to resting heart rate. For better accuracy you should take these changes into account.

High Intensity Endurance (HIE)

This is aerobic-capacity training. Its purpose is to increase the total amount of work you can do aerobically over a given period of time, building on your endurance base. Aerobic capacity is linked to aerobic power (see next page), in that it reflects the percentage of aerobic power that you can sustain for a prolonged period. Whereas aerobic power is largely determined by the stroke volume of your heart, aerobic capacity is increased by adaptations in the muscles you use for mountain bike riding. Both stroke volume and muscle adaptations affect and determine VO_2 max.

A HIE session is one of the hardest sessions in this book, demanding courage and high motivation, particularly if you attempt rides approaching and exceeding the 60-minute mark. Some elite-level riders have benefited from riding at their maximum effort for 100 minutes and more. The tough thing about this type of riding is that it is more steady-state riding than mountain biking, there is no respite; however, it is great for instilling the confidence you need to ride away from your opponents, secure in the knowledge that you can sustain a high pace. Bart Brentjens used this type of training in 1995 to put himself on the path to winning the mountain bike Tour de France (the Tour VTT) and the world cross-country championship.

HIE sessions are performed fractionally beneath lactate threshold. They can be motorpaced (as Brentjens did)...or in a paceline...or on your own...or a mixture of all three. The main goal is that these sessions have to be hard and relentless. If you're not familiar with motorpacing or paceline riding, it's time to find a friendly road racer and expand your appreciation of the road side of the sport. I expect that when road racers ask you about mountain biking, you do all you can to help them — so your karma should pay off here, right?

Flat terrain is better than hills, unless you can find one very long hill. The reason is that your pulse should be steady and not go over threshold level for periods longer than 30 seconds.

This session, if done for much longer than 30 minutes, will consume large chunks of your glycogen stores, which in turn will significantly increase recovery time. After a 60-minute session, glycogen stores in lesser-trained riders can take up to 24 hours to fully restock. So do not attempt any further training that relies heavily on glycogen as fuel until the next day. But that doesn't rule out hard training, because in build-up periods you can still do anaerobic work — although you need to take care in making the distinction between sessions at anaerobic and lactate-threshold levels. Always use your heart-rate monitor to confirm what heart-rate level you are training at. In any case, beware of overtraining. One of the symptoms of overtraining is a lower-than-expected heart rate when working out (as opposed to your resting pulse).

If you want to, you can break up a 60-minute block into four 15-minute repetitions, each separated by five minutes of easy pedaling. Some riders find it easier to do this than to keep going through a full 60 minutes; others find it hard to psyche themselves up for the next work period. If you are training in a group, the rest periods make a good time to reassemble.

HIGH INTENSITY ENDURANCE

INTENSITY: Race pace (75- to 80-percent heart-rate reserve max, although the most accomplished riders will be able to sustain 85- to 90-percent)

DURATION: 45-60 plus minutes

FREQUENCY: Not more than two times a week

TERRAIN: Paved roads better than dirt; flat or a long hill climb, but not undulating hills

TYPE/MAIN FUEL: aerobic/glycogen

CADENCE: 80-100 rpm

JUNIORS: 45-60 minutes; WOMEN: 30-60 minutes; NOVICES: 15-30 minutes

Aerobic Power (AP)

This is, in effect, your VO_2 max. It reflects the maximum amount of oxygen that you can utilize in a short effort to exhaustion. The way to increase your aerobic power is to increase the amount of blood your heart pumps out with each beat, a quantity commonly known as stroke volume.

This type of session increases the amount of work you can do without crossing the lactate threshold. During a race you will

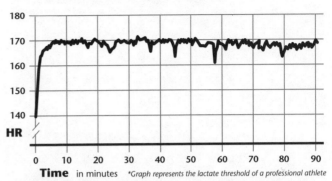

HIE: If MAX PR=180 LT=170

DIAGRAM 4.4 HIGH INTENSITY ENDURANCE

WARM-UP

The importance of warming up before starting a training session cannot be over-stressed, particularly for high-intensity training. A good warm-up not only increases your capacity for hard work, it also protects your muscles from injury. Warm muscle is more elastic, so it is less likely to tear when placed under heavy strain.

feel this benefit most when trying to catch a rider, or on steady climbs when the gradient increases for a few hundred yards.

Aerobic power training is great for increasing leg strength as well as cardiac stroke volume, and by performing it off-road on unfamiliar hills, you can also make important improvements to your skills. In other words, this is a very useful training session — not only for cross-country riders, but for downhillers as well.

At first, the hill should ideally take between four and six minutes to climb, and include some short pitches that may be too steep for your technique. Don't hesitate to include a short, technical pitch or two in your aerobic power training. This type of hill training provides excellent practice for your balance and concentration; however, not every power session should be like this. For best overall results, include a mixture of terrain (everything from gnarly dirt climbs to paved road hill climbs), putting the emphasis on paved-road riding.

Some coaches say that all aerobic power sessions should be on-road; although this may be true from a purely physiological standpoint, incorporating some of this type of off-road hill climbing is very good for increasing mental toughness and self-confidence, without the pressure of a race.

One of the main pointers for this type of session is to pedal slowly. Achieve this either by using a bigger gear or a steeper hill. Your cadence should not be higher than 60 rpm. This makes it harder for your legs, so be aware of the extra strain put upon connective tissue by the sheer mechanical forces involved. Be alert for any pain around the knee joints and pelvic-lumbar spinal regions. If you feel an injury coming on, stop the session immediately.

In the summary, I've listed repetitions of between four and six minutes. It's entirely up to you to choose which length of repetition you do. The reason for the wide range of terrain types is to adjust the AP training for the types of hills in your area, and to account for the possibility that you will be using several different climbs. I am not aware of any reason why fewer, longer reps would be any more beneficial to increasing aerobic power than more numerous, shorter reps.

Another important point: Don't turn on the stopwatch until your pulse has reached its 80-percent mark.

Keep in mind that you can also develop aerobic power with flat-course riding. Use the same duration, use a big gear and, if available, a head wind. Again, pedal cadence should not rise above 60 rpm.

Riding hard on the flat is very different to riding hard up a steep climb, and for this reason, it's a good idea to get in a few aerobic power sessions on flat terrain as well.

Recovery for both the uphill and the flat sessions is the same. Wait for your pulse to return to around the 50-percent mark. If this has not happened within six minutes, call it a day: Your body doesn't need such a hard workout.

AEROBIC POWER

INTENSITY: 80-85-percent heart-rate reserve max

DURATION: 4-6 minutes

FREQUENCY: 1-2 times a week

TERRAIN: On or off-road

TYPE/MAIN FUEL: aerobic stroke/glycogen

CADENCE: 60-80 rpm

AP heart rate trace

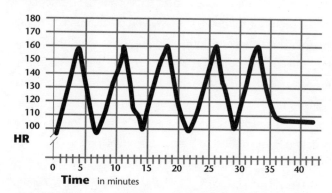

DIAGRAM 4.5 AEROBIC POWER (NUMBERS DERIVED USING HRR FORMULA)

If max HR=180, 80-85%=144-153 bpm. If you know your lactate threshold is at a higher HR, say 170, you can train up to that rate. In order to keep lactate build-up low, lactate threshold should not be surpassed. You might notice that in later reps HR does not drop to as low a level as in earlier reps. This is okay as long as you can get your HR up to the same high level each time.

Lactate Tolerance (LT)

Lactate tolerance means different things to cross-country and downhill riders. To downhill riders, lactate tolerance is what it is all about. Like 1500-meter runners, downhill racers must learn to love lactate. Having said that, like the 1500-meter foot race, downhilling is mainly an aerobically powered activity. High lactate levels are built up by that small fraction of the total work that is fueled anaerobically.

To cross-country riders, greater lactate tolerance means faster recovery on the descents and remaining functional for longer with increased blood-lactate levels. Although good lactate tolerance is essential for only small parts of the race, these are often the event's most important moments.

Lactate-tolerance training is possibly the most uncomfortable of all, and, as far as your muscles are concerned, it is the most destructive. It damages the aerobic enzymes, thereby reducing your aerobic power, and damages the muscle cell wall — which can ultimately result in minor leaks into the bloodstream.

This type of training is important, but because of its destructive effects, neither cross-country nor downhill riders should attempt it more than once a week. Remember, racing itself is also good lactate-tolerance training.

Lactate tolerance can be trained for in several ways. In Diagram 4.6, I've put down the most popular session, which involves short repetitions. Longer sessions also work; these sessions should last between 10 and 60 minutes.

The 10-minute session is very tough mentally as well as physically, and is not particularly useful for downhill racers. I find turbo trainers particularly good for this session; doing it in groups is even better because you can practice your poker face (first one to grimace buys the drinks). Sunglasses are permitted. In this session, you ride flat out for 10 minutes, pedal easily for eight, then go again. The first time you do a session, you do two repetitions; over a month's time you will build up to

LT heart rate trace — short intervals

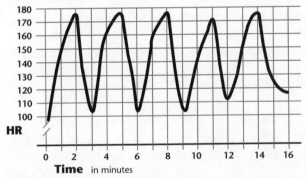

DIAGRAM 4.6 LACTATE TOLERANCE (NUMBERS DERIVED USING HRR FORMULA)
If max HR=180, 90%+=162+ bpm. HR in each repetition should surpass LT. During the session your recovery hr may show a gradual increase.

LT heart rate trace — long intervals

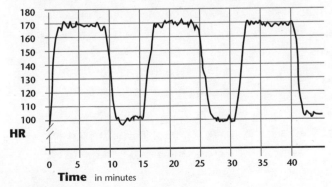

DIAGRAM 4.7 LACTATE TOLERANCE

five repetitions (three for juniors and novices, four for women and vets). Some riders may eventually do as many as 10 reps per session during the season, but that should be the limit.

If you want to do a longer session still, you could try entering a race and riding one or two laps above threshold intensity. Most riders (except some of the pros) will achieve this with a pulse of around 90-95 percent heart-rate reserve. I suggest doing this in a race, because it's difficult to motivate yourself to this level of training otherwise. Newcomers to the sport should make the hard lap(s) the final one (or two). More experienced riders should do a hard first lap, then ease back, and finally put in an extra-hard last lap. Races like this should be designated as training races, and you will obviously be more concerned about what your resulting heart-rate graph looks like than your race result.

Throughout all of your training, you should get used to asking yourself the question: Did that session work; did I accomplish what I set out to do? The diagrams below give a general idea of the heart-rate graphs produced by successful sessions of this type.

One final word: After a hard lactate-tolerance session, a day of rest or recovery riding is best. It's not unheard of for riders to take four days to fully recover from a hard LT session.

LACTATE TOLERANCE

INTENSITY: 90-plus percent heart-rate reserve

DURATION: 1-2 minutes per rep, with 30 seconds to 1 minute rest between reps

FREQUENCY: once a week, maximum

TERRAIN: on or off-road (uphill best), or turbo trainer

TYPE/MAIN FUEL: anaerobic/glycogen

CADENCE: 90-plus rpm

BREATHING: very fast rhythm

MINDSET: takes lots of concentration

Phospho-Creatine (PCr)

As this is mainly the sprinters' domain, you'd think there was no place for it in the cross-country rider's arsenal. But trials with cross-country ski racers — and anecdotal evidence from World Cup mountain bike racers — suggest that it is well worth training your PCr system. Look at it this way: PCr energy is what may get you over that steep lip or up that steep hairpin turn for which you'd otherwise have to dismount (and so lose valuable rhythm and time). Downhill racers need to have a well-trained PCr system, period.

Use a very steep hill that you find too long to crest in a single sprint. If you can find a new location each week, preferably with a different topography, so much the better. Making these short, sharp sprints, you can learn more about bike handling on very steep inclines, while you are training the energy system to power up them. If you do rely on a single training site, you will have the benefit of visible progress as your body starts to adapt to the training and you travel farther up the hill during the rep's duration.

If you are pushing yourself hard enough, you will know when the PCr in the muscles runs out: Your legs suddenly feel dead.

Effective PCr training is done with repetitions of between six and 10 seconds. You should allow a minimum of three minutes between repetitions, and five to six minutes between sets. Many track sprinters who use this type of training allow up to 10 minutes between repetitions. The reason for these long rest periods is to restore your creatine-phosphate supplies and ensure that blood lactate levels do not build up over the course of the training session. Some researchers believe that high blood-lactate levels delay the reformation of creatine phosphate. The number of repetitions you begin with will vary according to your age and experience. Beginners should start off with four repetitions,

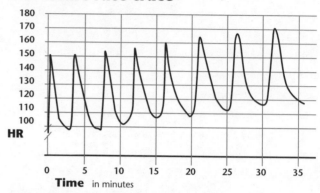

PCr heart rate trace

DIAGRAM 4.8 PHOSPHO-CREATINE

As the session progresses you will gradually come closer to your HR max. Quite possibly your recovery pulse will also gradually increase. As long as this increase is minor, and your graph shows a smooth, flat bottom between each exertion, that is okay. For this session to work it is essential that your heart rate is relatively low at the start of each sprint. Take more than four minutes recovery time if you want to.

and two sets. Raise the number of reps by two each session, until you reach 10, then add another set, starting at six reps. Perform this training for at least five weeks — more if you find it works well for you. Regarding the ceiling of repetitions, many riders consider three sets of 10 repetitions a good workout.

FARTLEK TRAINING

Fartlek training is not included in Table 4.1 because it doesn't readily fit into the grid. It is, however, ideally suited to mountain biking. The name comes from a Scandinavian word meaning "speed play," and the emphasis is equally on speed and play. In other words, you work hard, but it is an informal session with little structure. You go hard when you see something that looks good to go hard up — or down. The good thing about it is that you can do it practically all year round.

This type of training is supposed to be aerobic, so you shouldn't cross your lactate threshold during the intervals of hard work. In between intervals, wait at least long enough for your pulse to return to around 50-percent of HRR, which for many athletes is in the range 120-130 bpm. I see no reason why fartlek sessions cannot be performed at any time of the year. It is an effective form of non-specific training, in which you can work on skills as well as fitness. And the informality of it keeps an element of fun in your program. When you start fartlek sessions each year, the duration of the work intervals is about one minute and increases on a weekly basis by one minute until you have reached 10 minutes. After this there is not much point going on for longer, because then you get into High Intensity Endurance sessions.

Some physiologists think that occasionally shorter, more intense anaerobic exercise intervals can go into a fartlek session, and that not all intervals need to be as long as the longest one. However, if you do start to bend the rules by making these variations, make sure the general emphasis of the session remains based on aerobic intervals.

Downhill riders will benefit most from doing PCr training in three separate locations. Use the gears you'd normally use for racing on the selected terrain. First of all, practice starting sprints from a standstill. Second, start sprinting as you exit a corner. Third, practice on short uphills.

PHOSPHO-CREATINE

INTENSITY: maximum
DURATION: 10 seconds per repetition, 10-15 repetitions
FREQUENCY: once weekly
TERRAIN: off-road
TYPE/MAIN FUEL: anaerobic/creatine phosphate
CADENCE: 60-120 rpm
JUNIORS, WOMEN, AND NOVICES: Same as senior men

GROUP TRAINING

A note of warning if you are training in a group: Let your heart-rate monitor pace your effort. If your friend is pulling away, just accept it and work on your own training program — the tables might be turned next year. Another thing, unless one rider is using a heart-rate monitor with a disturbance-free transmission system, two riders with heart-rate monitors should keep at least two yards clear of one another to prevent the stronger transmitter signal from being picked up by both receiver units.

SUMMARY

❶ A good training plan will suit both your competitive aspirations and your lifestyle, and it should fit into the time you have available. An effective training plan also uses a variety of training sessions to develop all of your energy systems and increase your range of skills.

❷ For your training plan to be successful, you need to have feedback about your results. Feedback enables you to adjust the intensity, duration and frequency of your training sessions as you get fitter. Obviously, objective feedback tends to be more reliable than subjective feedback, particularly for less-experienced riders. This is why the next chapter details a number of methods for testing your fitness.

Chapter 5

Fitness-testing protocols

There is no such thing as a fixed training plan. Not one of them is fixed in stone like, say, the 10 Commandments. That's because, from time to time, everybody needs to make adjustments in their training schedule. These adjustments might be the result of gains in fitness or skill or, on the down side, the result of overtraining or periods of injury or disease. Exactly what, how much and when individual training exercises need to be changed are decisions you'll have to make as you go along. This is one of the reasons it takes years to become really good at training.

Fear not, however: There is objective help in determining physical fitness — one of the important factors in fine-tuning your training program. Fitness tests are widely accepted as a means of objectively monitoring the development of endurance and strength. Your training program will be the most effective if you can pinpoint your level of fitness. In other words, training works much better if, for example, what you believe is 80-percent of your heart-rate reserve really is 80-percent. Be forewarned: If your heart-rate estimations are off, you could end up wasting a lot of time, as well as overtraining.

This chapter explains additional measures to monitor your vital responses to training (both during and after exercise), and helps you assess the suitability of your training methodology. In an age where a variety of high-tech training methods are being touted by world-class athletes (mostly as advertisements), it is important to keep the basics in mind: regular checks of your general health (preferably by a qualified sports-medicine physician), and a strong desire to keep training. Problems in either area can quickly lead to burnout.

TIMING OF TESTS

Fitness tests are most effective at intervals of eight and 12 weeks. If you do them much closer together, your body might not have fully adapted to the changing exercise load. In between fitness tests, you need a way to monitor your desire to continue training and general day-to-day health. I recommend the *VeloNews* training diary because it has plenty of space to record this type of information.

I cannot overstress the good sense in a medical check-up, which should include a blood test, three months before the race season begins. This way your physician will have records that may come in useful. The ideal situation is to find a physician with a sports background. (A U.S.-contact source for sports-medicine physicians is listed in the "Useful Addresses" Appendix 1 at the back of the book.)

One of the most widely-used monitors of readiness for hard training and general fitness is your morning heart rate. The accurate recording of this involves an unhurried approach to

HEALTH WARNING

First, if you are over the age of 35 or have a history of health problems, you most certainly should seek the advice of a physician. Before undergoing fitness testing, make sure your physician fully understands that you will be involved in maximum-intensity exertion.

waking. The easiest and least-expensive method for taking your morning pulse is to place your fingers on your neck (on top of the carotid artery) and use a wristwatch to count the number of complete beats a minute. (see Table 5.1.) If you use this method of recording your pulse, be sure that you take the time to record the number in your training diary. A more accurate method of recording your morning pulse is to use a heart-rate monitor. Upon waking up, reach out for your chest strap transmitter and put it on. I suggest leaving the receiver-display unit on your bedside table, and make sure it is in memory-storage mode (if you have that option). Lie down again for five minutes or so and even drift off to sleep if you have time. Once you get up, review the heart-rate figures, and record the lowest in your training diary.

Test preparation and measurements

Training tests are notoriously difficult to conduct with any accuracy, but you can do a lot to improve the accuracy of the test by limiting the variables. The fewer variables, the better. Wind strength and direction, air temperature, air pressure, humidity, ground surface and gradient are some of the external environmental variables that you should try to standardize for any fitness test. Internal environmental variables (the ones going on inside your body) are affected by things such as diet and fluid intake, rest, sexual activity (mostly in men) and state of mind (depression, anxiety, stress, etc.). If any of these internal environmental variables are different than the

---

KEY FITNESS TEST MEASUREMENTS

① **Heart rate**

Universally expressed in beats per minute. How quickly does it respond to changing work loads? How does it coincide with various blood lactate levels? What is the highest heart rate and power output you can maintain over a 30-minute period? Over two hours? Resting pulse is also very important.

Heart rate is ideally measured with a heart-rate monitor, but if necessary it can be taken by gently pressing your index and middle fingers to the carotid artery (found about halfway between your windpipe and the start of your jaw).

② **Power output in watts**

If measuring equipment for this is not available, using your bike with a cycle computer and turbo trainer can yield useful speed and distance figures for comparison.

Power output or speed-distance indications are particularly relevant when related to heart rate.

③ **Blood lactate concentration and OBLA (Onset of Blood Lactate Accumulation) (lab test)**

Blood lactate level at given workloads can be very helpful in determining particular intensities for your training. If these levels are related to heart rate, as your condition improves you will find that you can work more intensely (i.e., at a higher heart rate) before your blood-lactate levels become intolerably high.

This test requires expensive equipment and trained personnel.

④ **VO$_2$ max (lab test)**

This is most useful to you and your trainer when related to power output (expressed in watts) or if on a turbo trainer, the maximum sustainable speed. VO$_2$ max shows how much work you can do aerobically.

This test also requires expensive equipment and trained personnel.

⑤ **Respiratory rate**

You could record this by having somebody count the number of times you breathe while working at a particular intensity. In fact, an accurate reading would be a meaningful indicator, provided criteria about respiratory volume could be provided.

Beyond this awkward kind of testing, your breathing rate tells you a lot about your level of exertion, and is a practical everyday test. You should become intimately acquainted with it, and I advise you to read appendix 2 on how breathing frequency and exertion are linked.

TABLE 5.1 THE KEY FITNESS TEST MEASUREMENTS

A LOOK AT THE SRM POWERCRANK®, COMPUTRAINER® AND KINGCYCLE®

The SRM Powercrank® is a converted crankset, invented in Germany, that is the most advanced pedaling output device commercially available. Among other things, it measures power output, heart rate, cadence, speed, distance and caloric expenditure.

Its main strength is that you simply put it on your bike, and away you go. At the end of testing, you plug the small handlebar unit into a personal computer to see the results.

The possibilities are huge. With an SRM, you can do comparative measurements on virtually any kind of in-the-field fitness testing.

The drawback is the price. At around $4500, the SRM is mainly limited to established coaches, clubs and riders with a lot of money to spend on training aids.

The CompuTrainer® was invented in the U.S., and consists of a turbo-trainer-like device for the rear wheel, a Nintendo unit, and some software. You'll need a television to make use of the visuals. The CompuTrainer® can measure power output, heart rate and endurance and can also diagram your pedal stroke, showing you where your strong and weak points are. It is useful for fitness testing and equipment testing, especially items like crank length. It is also useful for winter and bad-weather training, because it can provide simulated courses, giving you the illusion that you're riding that course. It can also simulate races for you by giving you a video-game-type competitor to race against.

The CompuTrainer® comes in two models, the first measures up to 1000 watts in power output and costs $1250. The second measures up to 1500 watts and costs $1500.

The King Cycle® is a British-invented, high quality turbo trainer attached to a computer. The main measurements it takes are power and heart rate.

The principal use of The King-Cycle® is to measure aerobic power, which reflects VO_2 max. In this test, which takes about 10 minutes, the cyclist watches a cursor on the computer screen and uses his or her gears and pedaling rate to keep it at a certain point. As time passes, the power output needed to do this steadily increases, and accordingly the rider changes into bigger gears. The test can be maximal or sub-maximal, with your heart rate being measured at a certain power output.

Price is in the $1500-$2000 region, without the computer.

The beauty of all these testing methods is that they allow you to use your own bicycle, although the CompuTrainer® and the Kingcycle® work better with a road bike, or at least smooth tires. See "Useful Addresses" Appendix 1 for more information on each of these items.

Outside of these options, you could contact a private human-performance laboratory or your national cycling federation. Several federations have testing and coaching facilities available for a reasonable fee. If your federation doesn't provide such a service, write them and ask them why not. Such response from members is very useful for national associations offering membership services.

personal norms you have recorded in your training diary, then I advise you to postpone any physiological test until you are back to "normal."

For more information on the key fitness-testing measurements, see Table 5.1.

HOW TO DO THE TESTS

I have listed a number of different test protocols in order to give you a sporting chance of finding at least one that you can use.

Laboratory tests are best for recording accurate results that you can compare with data collected on previous and subsequent tests; however, laboratory testing is out of reach for most cyclists. Lab tests are often free of charge to elite athletes, but lesser and up-and-coming riders usually have to pay, and specific tests tend to be prohibitively expensive. One way around this is to contact your local university exercise science department and volunteer as a subject in an endurance exercise experiment. You can then ask the lab technician to give you a copy of your results, but be forewarned that they may or may not be useful. Testing is mainly of value in monitoring your progress through a training schedule. So, a one-time test may be interesting, but doesn't offer much in the way of useable information.

Don't be discouraged. Reliable test equipment in the form of the SRM Powercranks, CompuTrainer and the Kingcycle is well within the price range of a club or a professional coach.

If the highly-skilled nature of mountain bike riding has you questioning the need for lab tests, because lab tests have no bearing on a real mountain bike course, I would say that you're right — to an extent. However, if I didn't believe that lab tests have at least some value, I wouldn't be mentioning them in this book. The good news is that there's a more accessible option (one that I expect the majority of you will turn to). Surprisingly useful data can be collected at home with a turbo trainer, a heart-rate monitor, a cycle computer and a helping hand. Since most of you will probably choose this option, I'll explain it first.

TESTS YOU CAN DO ON YOUR OWN
AEROBIC CAPACITY TEST
What is it for?
This test can substitute OBLA testing as a means of determining your lactate threshold heart rate. Many scientists and coaches have reported finding that a rider who sustains his or her maximum constant speed during a 30-minute period is exercising around his or her lactate threshold. Blood lactate tests have confirmed this.

If your heart rate dips or rises by more than five beats per minute, for a period of more than five minutes toward the end of the test, then you still need to make some adjustments to the starting intensity.

Once you've become accustomed to this test, and feel that you are putting everything into a sustained effort, you can take your average heart rate as representing your lactate threshold.
You will need:
One wind trainer that takes a mountain bike with a slick rear tire; one clock that records seconds; one cycle computer with sensors on the rear wheel; thermometer; a big fan if the temperature is warm — but even with a fan you should expect to see some cardiac drift. Cardiac drift occurs when the heart rate increases solely for the purpose of internal temperature

regulation. You will also need a pen, a note pad and a friend to make notes and offer encouragement. Have two water bottles filled with whatever you prefer to drink.

The test
This part is easy — for your assistant, that is. For you, it will be a session of self-inflicted pain, where willpower and the ability to put your mind elsewhere are your main allies. The test is tough physically and mentally, but it has the advantage of furnishing you with very good quality information about where your limit is at a particular time.

Do five to 10 minutes of pedaling to warm up, and some stretching if you want to. Minutes before the start of the test, your assistant will record the time of day, the temperature and what you are drinking. These factors could come in useful when analyzing your results.

When you are comfortable on the bike, make sure you can see the timing clock used by your assistant, although you will be told when to start and stop pedaling. On the word "go," accelerate rapidly to the maximum you think you can sustain for 30 minutes, and then hold it. The more frequently your assistant makes entries of your speed and heart rate, the better. A record put in every 20 seconds should provide a log sufficiently detailed to include all significant data. Your assistant should take care to record the exact distance shown on your computer at the finish of the test. This will help to reveal the constancy of your speed between each recording point.

This test should not be performed more often than once in a week. The first few times you perform this test, you might start too quickly and find your heart rate drops off in the last 15 minutes, or you might feel that you could have gone faster. It will probably take a few attempts before you can gauge your effort accurately; although, as you learn this skill, you will have a distinct advantage in both training and racing.

Test notes
① If you can do this test in an air-conditioned room, where the temperature is the same each time you do it, this would make the results more accurate. As I have said elsewhere in the book, when cycling in hot temperatures a higher proportion of your heart beats goes into keeping you cool.
② Although this test closely approximates your lactate-threshold heart rate, it's likely that the lactate quantities you generate in this test are greater than you will be able to sustain throughout a mountain bike race. For this reason, I do not recommend that you select this as your racing heart rate, which

should be between five to 10 beats per minute lower.

Details to record

• Pre-test: date, time of day, temperature, drink used, diet the day before, seat height, rider's body weight (wearing cycling shorts only — no shoes or socks), any special notes

• During test: heart rate, speed, both recorded every 20 seconds

• Post-test: distance covered during test, rider's body weight (This should be recorded before rider drinks any liquid following the test.)

CONSTANT-SPEED TEST

This variation on the above test is useful for more-frequent testing of your aerobic capacity. Again, you have to be aware of the variables, like time of day, wind, temperature, and so on.

Find a long climb, preferably on a paved road, and start from the same point each time. Perform the test by riding at a constant speed for one mile. Observe your heart rate as you climb. At a marked point soon after one mile, make a note of your heart rate. As your fitness improves over a period of a few months, you should see a progressive drop in your heart rate at the one-mile marker. If it is not improving, and all of the variables have been accounted for, you probably need to reduce the amount of high-intensity training you're doing.

LABORATORY TESTS

OBLA

What is it for?

Blood lactate concentration — that factor of exercise mentioned so often in Chapter 3 — serves as an effective basis for guiding the structure of your training sessions. Things would be a lot simpler if we could have a blood-lactate window, a bit like a Shimano gear-shift window, plugged into one of our forearms for easy reading.

Onset of Blood Lactate Accumulation is a slightly misleading term because even at rest you normally have at least some lactate in your blood. OBLA really refers to the point at which lactic acid concentration starts to build up rapidly in your blood and interferes with muscle activity (a more detailed explanation of this is given in Chapter 3).

Your lactate threshold is responsive to training stimulus, and to train most effectively you need to know the heart rate that coincides with your current lactate threshold. You can approximate this with the constant-speed test outlined above, or you can pinpoint it by going to a lab and paying for the test.

Relationship of Heart Rate, Blood Lactate Concentration and Power Output

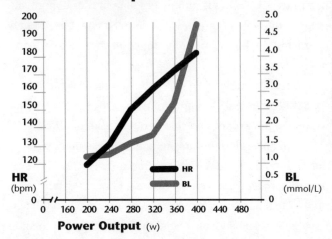

DIAGRAM 5.2 THE RELATIONSHIP OF HEART RATE, BLOOD LACTATE CONCENTRATION AND POWER OUTPUT

Note: Compare this graph to others you have obtained in the past to see how you are responding to training.

The test

Pinprick blood samples will be taken at regular intervals during a 15-20 minute test in which the intensity is stepped up every four to five minutes. Some time later, you'll receive a graph plotting power output, heart rate and blood lactate (see Diagram 5.2). The relationship of these three fitness indicators gives you a clear picture of your current level of fitness, and can suggest directions for further training.

The OBLA test is not necessarily as physically demanding as the do-it-yourself test described above, but the lab fees probably hurt more.

VO$_2$ MAX TEST

What is it for?

In very broad terms, VO$_2$ max is a fair predictor of performance in well-trained riders; however, it has almost no meaning to teenagers and newcomers to endurance sports, because physical characteristics can change very rapidly in these groups. The data from VO$_2$ max testing is less useful to endurance athletes than the data from OBLA testing, so if you have to choose between the two, OBLA is the better way to go. For more information on VO$_2$ max, see the discussion in Chapter 3.

The test

The test normally lasts between eight and 12 minutes, and you stop when you can no longer keep up the required effort.

Throughout the test, you breathe into a mouthpiece and wear heart-rate monitoring equipment. You will be presented a set of figures representing your maximum oxygen uptake at different levels of exercise, and another set of figures representing your power output in watts at each level.

FIELD TESTS

What are they?

For mountain bikers, field testing is perhaps the most relevant of all tests. A field test is simply a time trial over a given course and shows what you can do out there in the dirt. Field testing is also the best way to evaluate new equipment and riding techniques; however, external variables such as changing ground and atmospheric conditions can differ so much between one test and the next that the two sets of results are virtually incomparable. A roaring tail wind up a long climb can make a big difference, as can an unusually slippery surface on a big descent. If you are confident the external environmental variables are more-or-less constant, then go ahead and run the test. For the purpose of comparing data, it is a good idea to record as much information about the conditions as possible.

Whether you want to use this test as a fitness indicator, or

ABOUT HEART-RATE MONITORS

In this book I make frequent reference to heart rate. Your training would be more convenient if you were to acquire a heart-rate monitor. This is your most useful tool when it comes to gauging the amount of exercise stress you are putting on yourself. If you don't have access to one, then teach yourself to take your pulse while on the move (best done at the carotid artery in the neck).

Some riders express misgivings about heart-rate monitors. They say these devices take the fun and spontaneity out of a training session, and that they know their bodies well enough to get by without one. While that may be true for some of the most experienced riders, bear in mind that many leading pros use heart rate monitors in racing as well as training. All a heart-rate monitor does is accurately measure how fast your heart is beating. How can that spoil a ride? When wearing one of these electronic gadgets, you can be as creative and spontaneous as your heart desires, while at the same time your "mobile coach" gives you information about how hard you should work. Remember: Using a heart-rate monitor helps you work at the intensity that you decided on before you set out on your ride.

I wouldn't say that heart-rate monitors are infallible, because sometimes they do not concur with how a rider feels, but as a general tool for day-to-day information about what's going on in the internal environment, they are the best thing we have.

USING A heart-rate monitor

The three essential rates

① Resting
② Lactate threshold
③ Heart rate max

Regular recording and monitoring of these three heart rates will give you a good indication if you are maintaining fitness, gaining fitness, losing fitness or becoming ill.

Use in training

• Helps determine if you are truly taking it easy on easy days.
• Helps you determine if you are recovering properly between intervals
• Helps you stay within limits on hard days
• Provides an accurate record of training at different levels each week

Use in racing

• To give yourself that extra kick when you notice that your heart rate is down. (Juli Furtado reports using her heart-rate monitor this way.)
• Helps you determine your reserves. If you're with a group and you know you're comfortably inside your lactate threshold, then you know you can attack. If you see you're at your threshold, then you know that the attack is best kept until the last lap.
• Helps you to discipline yourself in the mad rush that inevitably happens on the first lap.

you want to use it to try a different technique, make sure you already know all the best lines and places to put in the big effort. Always stick to the same pattern when testing yourself so that no new factors affect the results.

The simple field test

This is quite simple: Use a heart-rate monitor and a stop watch, time yourself from an exactly marked start to an exactly marked finish, then compare heart rate and time with previous results.

The field test with an SRM Powercrank

Now we're talking. This is arguably the most useful testing device available to mountain bikes. So much of what is important comes down to power output. In addition to being an accurate instrument for recording and storing data about power output, the SRM Powercrank also records heart rate, distance covered, speed, cadence and a range of related data.

The Powercrank is particularly good for showing how your heart rate responds to a specified reduction in power output, such as going over the top of a hill. Because in-race recovery is so important in mountain biking, this type of information is very valuable, and you can use it to help map out your training priorities. Diagram 5.5 shows how such information might map out while riding and preparing for the 1996 Olympic mountain-bike course.

The SRM Powercrank is very useful at plotting power output against heart rate and distance against time, but it is also a great tool for determining which tire performs best under a certain set of conditions (mud, shale, rock, sand or a combination of terrain). This additional information concerning tires cannot help but give you a competitive edge, even if all you gain is the confidence of knowing that you have the best tires for the conditions. The Powercrank can also be used to test other pieces of equipment for racing, such as suspension or frame type.

At around $4000 a pop, the SRM system is too expensive for most individuals to buy for themselves, but this figure is well within the reach of a club, a trainer, or best of all a trainer attached to a club. Please don't tell me you're not a member of a club, I don't want to hear about it. It is to the advantage of all serious riders, particularly young riders, to be members of a racing club. So if you're not in a club, join one. If there isn't a club in your area, why not form one and make an important contribution to the sport? At the very least, cycling clubs give you a variety of riding partners, a feeling of camaraderie and the opportunity to race more often than you would on your own.

Power Output on Schöberer SRM

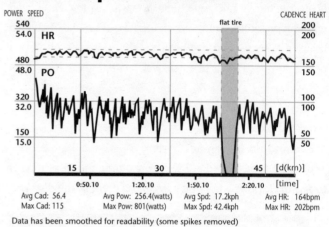

Avg Cad: 56.4   Avg Pow: 256.4(watts)   Avg Spd: 17.2kph   Avg HR: 164bpm
Max Cad: 115   Max Pow: 801(watts)   Max Spd: 42.4kph   Max HR: 202bpm

Data has been smoothed for readability (some spikes removed)

DIAGRAM 5.3 HEART RATE AND POWER OUTPUT TRACES FOR PROFESSIONAL RIDER AT PRE-OLYMPIC TRIAL, CONYERS, GEORGIA, 1995

DIETARY ANALYSIS

What is it for?

Although nutrition and diet are dealt with in Chapter 13, it's worth pointing out the value of going to a qualified nutritionist for a dietary analysis. The results often can be surprising. Most people consume a lot more fat than they think they do.

The process of recording your diet is anything but exciting: it involves recording and weighing all the food you eat in a one-week period. This makes food preparation quite a chore, as you need to record the dry weights of all your food, and the weight of the milk you put in your coffee and on your cereal. Although this is a nuisance at the time, the results are well worth the effort.

OVERALL APPROACH TO FITNESS TESTING

In Chapter 3, I explained how heart rate is a good indicator of your blood lactate levels. This means that by measuring your training heart rate, you can make a reasonable guess about how much lactate you have in your blood (a standard measure of training fitness). Chapter 3 also points out that heart rate is only a reliable indicator of blood lactate level if you regularly test your blood lactate levels to confirm the relationship between the two. (Everyone's body is different. "Regularly" means every six to eight weeks.)

As you progress through your training program, you can expect that at a given power output your blood lactate level and heart rate will get lower and lower. After training intensely for a certain period, you should find that you can maintain a higher heart rate (and blood-lactate concentration) for longer periods. On the other hand, in extended periods without training, you might find that your lactate levels become intolerably high at power outputs that were once manageable.

Although testing every six to eight weeks allows sufficient time for your body to adjust to training stimulus, remember that the test will only reflect what is going on in your body on that particular day, at that particular time. If you are feeling ill or going through some heavy-duty stress or grief, don't bother testing that day. One important factor often forgotten is diet. Standardizing your training and diet in the days leading up to a test makes the results a lot more meaningful when compared to past tests.

Fitness tests done every six to eight weeks can also be useful in goal setting. This time frame fits in particularly well with the time frames of medium-term goals. We'll discuss more about goal setting in the next chapter.

Chapter 6
Skills analysis and goal setting

The bike-handling skills required to ride a mountain bike over a cross-country or downhill course are a huge part of what makes this sport so challenging. Pursuing these skills should be an on-going project for any serious mountain bike racer, regardless of training or racing schedule, and I can't think of a classroom I'd rather spend time in. Easy training days during the racing season are the ideal time to turn yourself into a more-skilled rider.

If you belong to a club or have been around mountain bikes for a while, you already know that developing your bike-handling skills is part of the culture — something that's passed down through the ranks (even Hans Rey has his own instructional video). The rest of this chapter is filled with tips and exercises designed to make you a much better rider.

STRENGTHS AND WEAKNESSES

You'd be amazed by how much you can discover about yourself through listing what you are good at and what you are not (the scope of this exercise goes far beyond the confines of this book or mountain bike racing and riding). A surprising number of racers rely heavily on only one or two key strengths, rather than taking the time to maximize their all-around potential. However, cross-country and downhill racing demands that riders have a wide range of strengths, one or two truly outstanding qualities and no glaring weaknesses.

If you look carefully at pro racers, you'll find that most of them are basically sound in every aspect of mountain bike racing. Even if you're not in the same physiological shape as the pros, only one thing is preventing you from becoming a technically-adept all-round rider — you.

Depending on the kind of riding you do, cross-country or downhill, the following lists itemize the main components you need to learn.

TASK ANALYSES
CROSS-COUNTRY

Climbing
• long steep climbs
• short sharp climbs
• long gradual climbs

Transitions
• staying smooth through compressions
• gear selection for sudden ups or downs with obstacles

Descending
• single-track descents (both steep and gradual)
• fast descents
• scary descents (e.g., rocky drop-offs)
• jumps
• pre-jumps
• slowing down in a hurry when the going suddenly gets gnarly

Flat
• speed on smooth surface
• speed on bumpy surface
• sudden changes in pace (can also apply to climbs): increase or decrease
• sprints
• dismounting and mounting without losing speed or rhythm

General
• nutritional and fluid requirements
• avoiding mechanical problems and flats
• fast field repairs
• muscular flexibility
• riding at your own chosen pace

- last-lap energy
- reading the terrain and seeing the line
- knowing for how long you can exert yourself at particular intensities

DOWNHILL

Cognitive Skills

- reading the terrain and seeing the line
- near and far vision
- controlling start-line nerves

Physical condition

- pedaling courses
- short courses
- long courses

Smooth riding

- keeping the bike on the ground
- staying smooth
- not crashing (yes, *this* is a skill)
- technical courses

Cornering

- fast corners
- slow corners
- tight hairpin turns
- off-camber sections
- berms
- speed out of corners

Obstacles

- drop-offs
- water-bars
- jumps
- pre-jumping
- short uphills
- muddy conditions

General

- nutritional requirements
- muscular flexibility
- knowing for how long you can exert yourself at particular intensities

If you consider yourself to be deficient in several of these areas, relax; few riders outside the pro ranks can honestly tell you that they do not need work in a lot of these areas. This kind of knowledge does not come overnight, or through osmosis. Give yourself a few years and learn it all properly. With the help of this book, you can structure your learning so that you improve your

skills in as many areas as possible within each training session; for example, pick a course that requires you to negotiate 10 or more different types of obstacles. Then find several other courses, with the idea of not becoming too familiar with any of them. The secret to learning bike-handling skills is to practice often, but in small doses. By following a program of four half-hour sessions a week, I guarantee that you'll see dramatic improvement in your skills within a month.

You'll know that you've thoroughly learned a skill or technique when you automatically use it successfully on a trail that you are unfamiliar with. If you already have good skills and trail-sense, then push yourself to improve your skills by staying ahead of your training partners. By gradually performing these skills at a faster and faster pace, you will hard-wire them into your body, so you no longer think about how to hop over the log in front of you — you just do it.

Periodically refer to the above list to see what additions you've made to your skills repertoire.

GOAL SETTING

This section is derived from the work of the American sports psychologist, Richard A. Magill (*Motor Learning, Concepts and Applications*, WCB, Dubuque, 1989).

Two types of goals are likely to affect mountain bike racers. One of these is called an *ultimate goal*, which relates to your long-term performance. The other type is the *immediate goal*, which relates to your performance in short-term events such as a training session or a race. Both types of goals are essential when creating your overall training plan.

Goal setting is key to both learning and performance. When you have a skill to learn or refine, everything will go faster if you set yourself some realistic goals. For example, "I want to learn how to descend hairpin turns better before the start of the season. I am making a commitment to practice hairpins at least three times a week."

I've put down some notes about goal setting that should be useful for you.

- Difficult goals lead to better performance than easy goals, but the level of difficulty must be achievable. If the goals are too difficult, you'll get discouraged and quit giving it your all.
- Specific goals lead to better performance than do-your-best goals or no goals at all.
- Goal setting added to performance feedback (from a coach, team member or riding partner) is better than goal setting alone.

• Participant (that means you) involvement in goal setting leads to better performance gains than goals set without participant involvement, (i.e., by a coach). If you have a coach who uses goal setting, ask to be involved in setting those goals.

CURRENT SITUATION ANALYSIS

This exercise is one that you should do twice a year — once just before the racing season, and once just after it ends. To begin, copy or photocopy Diagram 5.1 and enter the following items across the bottom of the chart, according to your discipline.

CROSS-COUNTRY

1. long steep climbs
2. long easy climbs
3. short sharp climbs
4. compressions and big whoop-de-dos
5. single-track descents
6. long-race endurance
7. recovery after race
8. running
9. general technical skills (e.g., dismounting and remounting, handling unexpected obstacles, gaining time staying on the bike where others have to run)
10. reading the terrain and seeing the line
11. mud and rain
12. drinking during the race
13. gear selection
14. negotiating obstacles
15. overtaking on descents
16. recovery on descents
17. attacking over the hilltops

DOWNHILL

1. reading the terrain and seeing the line
2. controlling start-line nerves
3. pedaling courses
4. long courses
5. staying smooth
6. not crashing (once again, yes, this is a skill)
7. technical courses
8. fast corners
9. tight hairpins
10. off-camber sections
11. speed out of corners
12. drop-offs
13. water-bars

14. jumps
15. short uphills
16. muddy conditions
17. muscular flexibility
18. gear selection

One of my main goals here is to get you into the habit of thinking "what would be the best type of training for me: today, this week, this month, this year?" The suggestions I make throughout this book are race-proven and have been honed by my extensive work with professional mountain bike racers, but if you think you can come up with something that works better for you — go for it. Learning to trust your instincts is one of the best training tools you'll ever acquire (and one I can't teach you).

Once you've listed the above items across the bottom of the grid, enter a 1-to-5 scale vertically up the side. A "5" means you are very strong in this area, while a "1" means that busloads of people were passing you in your last race, suggesting ample room for improvement. A score of "3" means you hold your ground in relation to the overall race.

Fill in the chart, marking a dot corresponding to the 1-to-5 scale for each of the items. If you end up with a solid row of 5s across the bottom of the chart, try doing it again tomorrow when you're thinking properly. If you still get these scores, it may be worth getting a training partner, friend, or coach to offer an objective opinion on your self-assessment.

Next, you decide, preferably with the help of an objective second opinion, how far you think you can reasonably expect to improve in each of these categories by the end of your racing season. Write down these "long-term" goals on another photocopy of the chart and mark it *ultimate goals,* and staple the two sheets together. When you re-evaluate yourself at the end of the season, you'll be able to measure how successful you've been at setting and achieving your goals.

CROSS-COUNTRY HYDRATION

A note to cross-country riders: with respect to drinking, a score of "5" means you sip a carbohydrate and electrolyte solution, approximately every 10 minutes throughout the race, and are well hydrated before the start. A "1" score means that you take a bottle of "something or other" along in case you get thirsty.

The same system of analysis holds true for immediate goals; the only difference is the length of time between evaluations. With immediate goals, you may want to re-evaluate your progress every week, every race or every month. You make the call.

If, for the purpose of streamlining your immediate goal setting, you want to undergo a full-skills analysis again, say halfway through the season, by all means do so. However, if you are going to the trouble of doing another skills analysis, I strongly recommend going all the way, and not just re-evaluating your descending, or trench hopping skills. Strength, endurance, flexibility and bike-handling are all skills that can be learned and improved upon.

Allocating available time

Wait until you have put in a couple of weeks' worth of training before you come up with a serious training plan. A training plan is only as useful as it allows you to improve your skills within the limited time you spend on your bike. Becoming a slave to some masochistic training regime is a recipe for burnout. The first thing you should do is jot down the number of hours available for training on each day of the week, then determine how many hours you'll have for practicing your strengths and weaknesses.

For the first half of the off-season, as much as 50-percent of your training time should go into skills training, with 70-percent of that time spent on weaknesses and 30 percent on strengths. (A strength is anything with a "4" or "5" score in your analysis chart.) As the race season approaches (one to two months away), do as much skills training as you can fit into your training schedule, because at this point in the off-season your main push is getting your physical condition right. With the 70-30 split, you'll stay on top of your strengths, while your weaknesses gradually turn into strengths.

Designing your race calendar

Winning a mountain bike race ain't easy: That's why only one person out of all the starters wins. Many of the starters have the potential to win, but when it comes down to it, only one has enough mental toughness, physical condition, and range of skills to win (I don't count mechanical problems in this because many of them are avoidable).

If you find that you're always being beaten by superior riders, you'll never develop the confidence necessary to go it alone after launching a devastating attack; likewise, if you only pick races where you're favored to do well, you'll be intimidated by the big events and ride below your abilities. As with many things

in life, the answer lies somewhere in the middle: you need to select some races against superior riders, to learn from them and work out your weaknesses, but you also need to enter some races where you can have a chance at a podium placement.

For downhill racers, the best advice is fairly simple: make sure you compete on a variety of courses and at different levels of competition, but the majority of the courses you race on should be very technical, rather than pedaler's courses. As you improve your downhill skills, you'll find that the best racers in the world excel on technical courses, and that the World Cup and world championships are set up to test a rider's technical skills. So if you want to race with the big kids, you have to start racing like them.

Self-discipline and your training plan

As far as training is concerned, there are only three valid excuses for missing a session: illness, fatigue and lifestyle change. Nothing else justifies missing a session. If you find you're getting stale, or have too many other commitments, then you may have to change your training schedule, but a decision to alter your training schedule should only be made after much soul-searching.

As a racer, your training plan is your foundation — so make it solid. Sticking to your training plan won't make you a great racer, but if you don't stick to your plan, you'll miss out on a ton of valuable feedback. If your training plan is sound, you'll see results that indicate what works and what doesn't. Without that feedback, you might as well just go out and ride. Enough said.

Now you need to take a lot of care and time designing a training plan that works for your lifestyle. Learning how to design a training plan might take five years or more, so enjoy the journey. If you're willing to learn, perfecting a training plan may teach you more about your body and yourself than anything you've ever done.

Most people start off trying to do too much. This is a perfectly natural mistake, and one that I have made myself. It is a lot better to start off with a program that is too easy and leaves you hungry for more, with spare time for other things, than it is to overtrain and burn out.

For many beginner and less-serious riders, I suggest designing a very flexible, undefined training plan, so you remove the risk of letting yourself down by not sticking to it. It could be something like this: a race or else a hard ride on the weekend, then two training rides during the week, one of which is two hours steady and the other of which is half-an-hour flat out. This is a schedule that will give you flexibility and enough fit-

ness to enjoy racing in the novice and possibly the sport class
— after a season's introduction. This is the sort of schedule I
use myself, as a busy 33-year-old, former elite-class racer who
still enjoys racing now and again.

As your aspirations and skills increase, you may want to set
tougher training goals. Whatever you do, don't design a plan
that demands a big alteration to what you are doing now —
that is the surest route to frustration and disappointment. If
you don't already know it, one important aspect of mountain-
bike racing that applies equally well to life is that change is
only effective if it's gradual.

SUMMARY

Competence on the bike depends on clearly definable skills.
Developing these skills is much more effective when you set
goals and chart your progress. While it's important to work on
improving your weak areas, you should also do basic maintenance on your strengths.

When it comes to setting your race schedule, plan plenty of
"training" races, which you enter to have fun and a hard workout, as well as to practice new skills that you're working on.
When mapping out these "training" races, find ones that give
you a variation in the terrain and level of competition.

It's all too easy to start dreaming and get unrealistic when
designing training schedules. Take the time to create a schedule that works for you and your lifestyle. Your training schedule has to be something you can stick to, because not sticking
to it will cause you stress. For this reason alone, all the extra
time you invest in designing a complete training program will
be time well rewarded.

The next chapters will specifically show you when to do what
kind of training, and for what purpose. Chapter 7 outlines the
concept of periodization, and then Chapter 8 covers the cross-
country training year, while Chapter 10 covers the downhill
year. Even if you practice only one of these disciplines, I encourage you to read both chapters. The knowledge applied to one
discipline may help you solve a problem in the other. Or, to
put it another way, if a little knowledge is a dangerous thing,
you'll be safer this way.

Chapter 7

Periodization

Once upon a time, raw talent might have been enough to get you to the top of the sports pinnacle, but in these days of scientific training and big-dollar athletics, making it on talent alone seems like a romantic throwback to a bygone era. Even if you are only interested in competing at the novice or sport level, a working understanding of training theory will go a long way toward improving your performance and preventing injuries and overtraining. The best way to utilize all the hours you spend training is to create some kind of schedule — a training plan. Instinctively, most people already have a training plan, even if they don't know it. If all you do is gradually increase the number of hours you spend training before the season, peak your training in the middle of the season, and taper off toward the end, then you have a training program.

All training programs, even the simplistic one I just outlined, are based on the concept of periodization: There are times to go hard and times to take it easy. Periodization training has actually been around almost as long as sports have, which just goes to show you that a lot of what falls under the heading of "Sports Science" is merely common sense. When you are setting up any training program, don't get carried away with grandiose plans; use your common sense about how much (frequency) and how hard (intensity) you can train in a given period.

I would like to acknowledge the work of Tudor O. Bompa, widely considered one of the world's leading authorities on planning and periodization in sport. Much of the material presented in this chapter is derived from his work.

WHY PERIODS

At the time this book was printed, the best scientific infor-

A PLAN & A DIARY ARE ESSENTIAL

Not having a training plan could be compared to trying to sail across the Atlantic without any nautical charts. If you do not keep a training diary, then it is extremely difficult to correlate your fitness and performance with your training; the only thing you have to go on is how you feel, which may be an important subjective gauge, but it offers little in the way of objective information. You need to know exactly what you did in your training and what the results were. Without this information, you might as well be lost at sea. No serious racer, especially in his or her developing years, should consider training without a training plan or a diary.

mation available indicates that maximum fitness development takes place in a cyclical pattern — periods of increasingly hard work, interspersed with periods of rest and lighter workloads. These periods, or "macrocycles," are blocks of time that begin at about four weeks and go up from there. Every periodized training plan contains several layers of training, which are designed to gradually introduce your body to more intense work. Each macrocycle has a particular purpose, as does the position of each layer or sub-period within a macrocycle. The order of these layers is crucial to maximizing your potential for sustained high-intensity endurance exercise. Each layer within a macrocycle corresponds to a different energy system.

So, by simultaneously training several different layers within one cycle, you can develop different energy systems, which in turn improves your performance.

Because the laws of biomechanics do not allow you to sustain the highest level of athletic fitness throughout the year, the periodized approach to training helps you build toward peak form in the second half of the racing season, when most of the really important races take place. Think of the total energy you have for the season like a checking account. You get paid once a month, so there is money (energy) going into the account, but if you blow all your paycheck by the 15th of the month, then there might not be anything left to pay your bills. However, if you spend your money wisely, you've got something left over every month ... you get the idea. So, if you follow a macrocycle of intense or high-volume training with a period of regeneration, you will enable yourself to perform at a higher level of intensity later in the year.

By combining the principle of progressive load (intensity) and volume (frequency) with that of regeneration, we can see the emergence of a stepped pattern of training and performance, as shown in Diagram 7.1. This graphic is a template for a long and rewarding career in racing at any level.

General phases in a periodized training plan:

① Preparation

    a) general preparation

DIAGRAM 7.1

The general plan of periodization follows a basic route: ① preparation, ② racing, and ③ transition. The phases of preparation and competition can be sub-divided into two further phases: General and specific preparation; and pre-competition and competition. Each phase is split into smaller parts, called macro-cycles, which normally last between four and six weeks. Macro-cycles in turn comprise even smaller cycles, called micro-cycles, which are of flexible duration based around one week.

    b) specific preparation

② Racing

    a) pre-competition

    b) competition

③ Transition

Each of these three general phases of the training year can be broken down into macrocycles, which normally last between four and six weeks. Macrocycles, in turn, can be broken down into smaller units called "microcycles," which normally have a flexible duration of approximately one week.

The order of sequencing in cross country and downhill mountain bike racing involves the following components:

Endurance

Strength

Speed

Power

Anaerobic fatigue resistance

Main racing season

Transition

As you can see in Diagram 7.2, some of the components are developed simultaneously. This is particularly important in the case of power. It is commonly accepted among exercise physiologists that maximum overall power occurs when speed and strength are developed independently of each other. In the Conversion period, speed and strength are blended along with endurance to produce a specific type of power that is sustainable for up to several minutes at a time. This is exactly the kind of power that a successful mountain bike racer needs at his or her command.

One of the most important aspects of a training plan is flexibility. Without the built-in understanding of flexibility, a training plan could quickly degrade into something akin to the

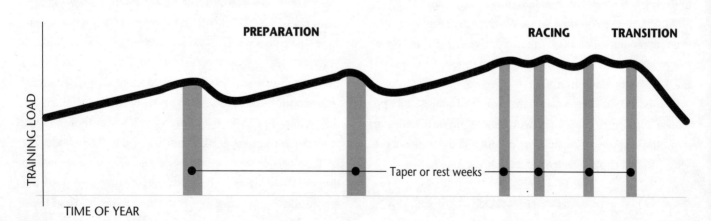

MONTH	11	12	1	2	3	4	5	6	7	8	9	10
PERIOD/TYPE OF TRAINING	General preparation		Specific preparation		Early season competition			Main season competition				Transition
ENDURANCE	Easy and moderate aerobic		High intensity aerobic		Anaerobic endurance		Specific endurance					Recreation
STRENGTH	Low intensity and high repetitions			Maximum strength		Conversion		Maintenance				General
SPEED	Fartlek		Speed and pedaling ability					Fartlek				General

DIAGRAM 7.2
The year divided into periods, broadly outlining what to do and when. The allocation of space (time) given to strength, endurance and speed work gives a rough idea of the relative importance of these fitness components in mountain bike racing.

Spanish Inquisition. Your rate of progress is the ultimate influence on your decision to increase the level of training. Regardless of what your training plan dictates, if you're not ready to make the step to the next level of training, don't do it. Let your body guide you on. If you feel totally exhausted the morning after a hard training ride, then you need to back off. Injury and inexperience are also legitimate reasons to alter a training plan. Obviously, if you're injured then you can't train, at least not at 100-percent. If you lack the experience to progress any faster than you already are, don't worry about it. Just continue to put in the time; the results will come — perhaps not as fast as you would like.

The chronological order in Diagram 7.2 is not fixed. The duration of each period depends upon how much experience you have and your readiness to progress into uncharted territory. Your age and whether you are male or female is less important in this regard than your willingness to step it up a bit. All training referred to in Diagram 7.2 starts in month 11, and goes through to the start of the season's main competition. During the main season, strength is maintained in biweekly sessions. Endurance and fartlek training should also take place two-to-three times a week.

Novice, Juniors and Sport

The following guidelines apply not only to beginners but to all junior racers, regardless of experience. I see far too many juniors taking shortcuts. A more illustrious career awaits the junior who has the willingness to undergo a comprehensive base of training — a foundation.

In this category, I recommend shooting for a relatively short Main Competition period. Ten weeks is plenty. You are likely to be racing before that, but this racing is still considered training and any good results you gain in this period should be counted as a bonus. The build-up for the Main Competition should follow these guidelines:

ENDURANCE
Low-intensity endurance (LIE) — 16 weeks
High-intensity endurance (HIE) — 12 weeks
Lactate Tolerance (LT) — 4 weeks
STRENGTH
Basic strength — 12 weeks
Maximum strength — 12 weeks
Conversion to sustainable power — 6 weeks
SPEED
Fartlek training — 16 weeks
Specific speed and agility — 14 weeks

Sport, Expert and Elite

Riders with several seasons' worth of racing experience will not enjoy significant fitness gains by prolonging the basic levels of training. In these classes of racing, the edge is gained by lots of hard work honing specific energy systems and having a longer competitive season. Riders at this level will pay close attention to technique, particularly while performing high-intensity work.

The build-up for the Main Competition should follow these guidelines:

ENDURANCE

  Low-intensity endurance (LIE) — 10 weeks

  High-intensity endurance (HIE) — 10 weeks

  Lactate tolerance (LT) — 6 weeks

STRENGTH

  Basic strength — 10 weeks

  Maximum strength — 8 weeks

  Conversion to sustainable power — 6 weeks

SPEED

  Fartlek —16 weeks

  Specific speed and agility — 14 weeks

Other Considerations

When devising your training plan, you need to consider the climate and calendar seasons in your particular geographic area. You don't have to be a genius to figure out that climatic conditions dictate much of your training activity. For example, in areas that receive a heavy winter snowfall, cross-country skiing, ski-skating and running will probably form the base of your endurance training, while indoor sports like basketball, volleyball, hockey, martial arts and weight training form the base of your motor-control training.

SUMMARY

Periodization helps map out your training year, and helps you keep your training on-track, yet allows you to stay flexible enough to cope with your individual rate of progress and unexpected obstacles like injuries. Progressive, sequential training is widely accepted as the best means of producing top form at the peak of the racing season. This chapter has made a brief introduction of the concepts behind the periodized year. For more information about how to put a training plan together, see Chapter 4.

Chapter 8

The cross-country year

As with any major project, putting together an annual training plan requires a certain level of organizational skills, but the payback, in terms of direction and focus throughout the year, is as good as money back on your investment. Putting one of these plans together is a big job. It will probably take up all of the dining-room table, most of the day, several cups of coffee, and lengthy consultations with your partner and other family members about work/school schedules, weekends, vacations and other planned holidays. Oh, and by the way, you'll almost certainly need a crystal ball.

Seriously though, it is both inspirational and useful to make educated guesses about what you might be doing several months down the road, particularly when it comes to deciding on the week when you want to be in your peak form for the year. Unfortunately, life has a way of changing all your best-laid plans with one fell swoop (and then changing it all back again two weeks later). With this in mind, long-term plans should be drawn up as general guidelines, and not as fixed entities that are impervious to change.

So you may ask, "Why bother creating such a detailed chart at all?" The answer is that it gives you something to shoot for, and shows you what a detailed training plan looks like. I know you wouldn't consider traveling in a place you had never been before without some kind of map; the same goes for training. A training plan is a map designed to take you from where you are to where you want to be; it's also a non-linear chart that is built on blocks of time, approximately six weeks long. As

you progress through the year, each six-week block of training gives you more information on how to fine tune your training in the weeks to come.

At the end of the year, you can use the chart as a tool to evaluate this year's training, and as a benchmark for next year.

The purpose of this chapter (and this book) is to provide you with the basic principles of training and the knowledge necessary to monitor your own training progress. With practice, you should be able to understand what your body is telling you — whether the training is too much or not enough — and, most importantly, how to avoid being carried away to the land of overtraining on the wings of enthusiasm.

The annual training overviews in Diagrams 8.1-4 lay out some skeleton structures that have been tried and tested on a mixture of sport and elite class riders. The unavoidable truth about any sensible training plan is that you have to work out the details for yourself.

DETAILS YOU WILL NEED TO WORK OUT FOR YOURSELF

- your exact heart rates at the different levels of intensity;
- when you are ready to progress to a greater intensity, frequency and/or duration of training;
- whether you want a particular training session to be a clinical set of repetitions on a hillside or an uplifting experience in The Great Outdoors — or a mixture of the two;
- how much time you can devote to training (I have suggest-

ed weekly hour totals that range from beginner to elite level competitors).

Please refer to Appendix 6 (page 110) for charts 8.1-8.4

NOTES ON THE SUGGESTED TRAINING PLANS

None of the following training plans is designed to be carried out to the letter. I've included them to give you an idea about the shape and sequence of training exercises.

The details given below take a keyhole view at particular periods. I recommend adjusting to the figures given in the graphs above, but whether you increase or decrease depends upon where you are in the season. In the earlier stages, you would expect to do a lighter volume, and you may want to increase the volume or intensity later in the season. In Diagrams 8.2 and 8.4, I have made suggestions on how to vary the High Intensity Endurance sessions. These will give you the general flavor of the kinds of alterations I am talking about.

If you are a fit and healthy person, you shouldn't have any problems following the suggested programs. If you have any doubts about or problems with your health, consult a medical practitioner before you do any further planning.

XC PLAN 1

Beginners, Juniors, Sport, Women, Masters

GENERAL PREPARATION PHASE

Day of Week/Training Aim	Exercise Options *(Choose any one you like)*
SUNDAY 2 hours LIE	mtb, xc ski, run, hike, aerobics, gym work-out
MONDAY 45 min HIE	mtb, xc ski, run, aerobics, gymnastics, wrestling, trampolining
TUESDAY 45min Fartlek 1 hour LIE	mtb, xc ski, run as above
WEDNESDAY 45min HIE 1 hour LIE	as above as above
THURSDAY 2 hours LIE	as above
FRIDAY 45min Fartlek	as above
SATURDAY	DAY OFF

Aerobic Power sessions performed during this period should be done on a bicycle, either outside or indoors on a turbo trainer. The shortened HIE sessions can be done in any of the ways suggested above.

SPECIFIC PREPARATION PHASE

Day of Week/Training Aim	Exercise Options
SUNDAY 1 hour HIE	On bicycle (if not possible, then on skis or running. If still not possible after two weeks, use a turbo trainer)
MONDAY 45min REC	as above
TUESDAY 45min AP	on a bicycle, either outside or on a turbo trainer
WEDNESDAY 2 hours LIE	On bicycle (if not possible, use xc skis or running. If still not possible after two weeks, use a turbo trainer)
THURSDAY 1 hour HIE	as above
FRIDAY 1 hour HIE 0.5 hour PCr	as above on a bicycle, either outdoors or a turbo trainer
SATURDAY	DAY OFF

EARLY-SEASON COMPETITION

Day of Week/Training Aim	Exercise Options
SUNDAY *(If not racing...)* 1 hour HIE	pref. off-road
MONDAY 45min REC	pref. on-road
TUESDAY 2 hour LIE	30 min. Lactate Tolerance (This is the starting point. During this month you would build up by 10 to 15 minutes each session.)
WEDNESDAY 1 hour LIE 45min	Aerobic Power
THURSDAY 45 min REC	pref. on-road
FRIDAY 1.5 hour HIE 45 min PCr	pref. on-road paying special attention to pedaling style
SATURDAY	DAY OFF

EASY WEEKS

Note: You won't get a complete rest here, but it is a lull that some find a welcome and needed break (for reasons of psychological refreshment as much as physiological recuperation).

You should do one session of High Intensity Endurance for 1 hour, and one Fartlek session for 1 to1.5 hours.

MAIN SEASON COMPETITION

Day of Week/Training Aim	Exercise Options
SUNDAY Race or 1.5 hour HIE	pref. off-road
MONDAY 1 hour REC	pref. on-road

TUESDAY 1.5 hours HIE	preferably on-road
WEDNESDAY 1.5 hours Fartlek	off-road
THURSDAY 45min PCr	off-road
FRIDAY 1 hour skills training	off road
30 min LT	on-road
SATURDAY	DAY OFF

TRANSITION

The main purpose of this period is to relax and regenerate after the racing season. If you cannot bear the prospect of exercise, don't do any. But it is far better for you to do light exercise in this period. Do whatever you want to, really. This is the time to catch up on all those other activities that you used to love to do before you got into mountain bike racing: canoeing, surfing, volleyball, ultimate Frisbee, rock climbing, in-line skating ... you name it. But keep in mind the main thing is to relax, kick back and enjoy yourself.

XC PLAN 2

Expert/Elite Men and Women; Sport Men; Veteran Men

If the volume of high-intensity training appears very high, please consider that the times suggested are those for the complete session, including recovery time in between repetitions and intervals (see Chapter 4 "Intro to Training Programs").

GENERAL PREPARATION PHASE

Day of week/Training Aim	Exercise Options
	(a mixture is suitable,
	e.g.: 1 hour run, 2 hours xc ski)
SUNDAY	
MONDAY 1:45 hours Fartlek	mtb, xc ski, run, aerobics, gymnastics, wrestling, trampolining
TUESDAY 2 hours LIE	mtb, xc ski, hike, aerobics, gym work-out
WEDNESDAY 1 hour HIE	mtb, xc ski, run, aerobics, gym work-out
THURSDAY 2 hours LIE	as above
FRIDAY 3 hours LIE	as above
SATURDAY	DAY OFF

SPECIFIC PREPARATION PHASE

Day of Week/Training Aim	Exercise Options
SUNDAY 2 hours HIE	mtb or on-road if snowy or wet
MONDAY 1 hour REC	on-road

40 min PCr	on or off-road
TUESDAY 2.5 hours LIE	on or off-road
1 hour AP	on or off-road
WEDNESDAY 1 hour HIE	on or off-road
40 min LT	turbo trainer
THURSDAY 1 hour AP	on or off-road
FRIDAY 1 hour HIE	on or off-road
40 min LT	turbo trainer
SATURDAY	DAY OFF

If a high intensity session follows a long steady, or hard ride, take along an extra bottle with a rich carbohydrate solution (7% to 15%), which you should drink as your first bottle. This will help you in the harder session.

EARLY SEASON COMPETITION

Day of Week/Training Aim	Exercise Options
SUNDAY *(If not racing)*	
2 hours HIE	off-road
30 min LT	off-road
MONDAY 1.5 hours REC	on-road
TUESDAY 1.25 hours LIE	on or off-road
	(may include skills training)
40 min AP	on or off-road
WEDNESDAY 1.5 hours HIE	on-road
1 hour LT	on or off-road
THURSDAY 1.5 hours REC	on-road
FRIDAY 1 hour HIE	on or off-road
30 min LT	
SATURDAY 45 min PCr	off-road

In this period you can count racing as training hours.

MAIN SEASON COMPETITION

Day of Week/Training Aim	Exercise Options
SUNDAY	RACE
MONDAY 1 hour REC	on-road
TUESDAY 1.5-2 hours HIE	on-road
WEDNESDAY 1 hour HIE	on-road
1 hour LIE	off-road (skills practice)
THURSDAY 1.5 hours Fartlek	off-road
FRIDAY 1.5 hours HIE	on-road
SATURDAY	DAY OFF

TRANSITION

The main purpose of this period is to relax and regenerate

after the racing season. If you cannot bear the prospect of exercise, don't do any. But it is far better for you to do light exercise in this period. Do whatever you want to, really. This is the time to catch up on all those other activities that you used to love to do before you got into mountain bike racing: canoeing, surfing, volleyball, ultimate Frisbee, rock climbing, in-line skating ... you name it. But keep in mind the main thing is to relax, kick back and enjoy yourself.

GETTING DOWN TO PLANNING

Now it is time to design your program. You might want to insert a few bookmarks in the following chapters for ease of reference.

Chapter 4 outlined the training sessions: What each does and how they should be approached. Chapter 5 introduced fitness-testing protocols, which allow you to make adjustments to your training heart-rate zones as you get fitter. In Chapter 6, we looked at goal setting and a way of analyzing your strengths and weaknesses. In Chapter 7, we saw that the year is divided into periods of greater or lesser training loads, and a path of gradual progression is followed.

A really high-class training program puts the ideas presented in these chapters together into one comprehensive and reasoned plan for continuing improvement. The initial laying out of such a plan might take up the better part of a day, but the reward is that you have something that is basically sound and can be referenced any time you want to. Devising a training plan that really clicks for you can take years of fine-tuning. Still, there is no better time to start than right now.

STEP ONE

Your master plan. To set this, return to Chapter 6 and follow the instructions. This gives you an idea of what you will be working on during several of your weekly sessions. Wherever you can, double up, so you train fitness and bike skills in one exercise.

STEP TWO

Make a rough fitness-training scheme along the same lines as Diagram 7.1. It is important to leave spaces to write in the skills you want to train in specific weeks or periods.

STEP THREE

Review your current situation analysis and fill in the skills you want to practice. This part should be planned no more than six weeks in advance, because it is heavily dependent on the rate at which you acquire new skills. Give priority to your weak points.

STEP FOUR

Work out how much time you are going to have available, and when you will be involved with other things such as family holidays and travel assignments. Some of you will be able to ride to and from work as part of your training effort.

NOTES ON FITNESS TRAINING

• If performing consecutive hard days, which you can do in cycling, work on different energy systems from one day to the next. Otherwise you risk over-stressing a system (see Chapter 3: "Physiology, Principles of Fitness & Training").

• Avoid overtraining! If you feel the approach of overtraining symptoms, or you are simply unable to complete the training sessions, take a week off training altogether. In particular, reduce the volume of high-intensity sessions. One simple way to do this is by shifting to a 14 day cycle, instead of the seven-day programs I have outlined. After each day involving a repeat or interval session, do a day of low-intensity endurance or recovery riding. For some riders, this might prove to be a more successful format right from the start, so be prepared to experiment. Just make sure to record everything in your *VeloNews* training diary.

• The pattern of training variation suggested in Diagrams 8.2 and 8.4 is only a suggestion. If you don't feel ready to step up a to a higher volume, don't try to keep up with the suggested schedule. Go at your own pace. Remember, I have no idea how you respond to training. This is one reason why it is always better to work with a good coach — this person can control your rate of progress, help balance your program and help you through a whole range of problem areas.

• If you are serious enough and experienced enough to train twice a day, here are some general guidelines:

① After your first session, put on dry clothes, eat, hydrate, shower, rest (get a massage if possible) — in that order. After the second session, you might want to shower first, but if you are training as hard as this, the sooner you can eat after exercise the faster your recovery will be.

② Normally you won't do two hard sessions in one day. If you do, make one of them relatively brief, such as creatine phosphate and lactate-tolerance training (If you mix lactate tolerance with another type of training in a day, do the lactate tolerance work as the later session).

③ During the race season, try not to fully deplete your glycogen stores in training. Once a week is more than enough exposure to glycogen depletion, and this will likely happen in a race.

If you do deplete your glycogen stores within four or five days of a race and continue hard training in the days following, chances are you won't be 100 percent come race day. While this is not necessarily a bad thing, if done with care during periods of heavy build-up training, you should avoid this kind of training in the mid-to-late race season. In this period of high-intensity sessions, one hour is quite adequate as aerobic training, even for pro level racing, and take less recovery than longer sessions.

SUMMARY

To put together an effective training schedule, it requires a lot of time and thought. In so doing, you must accurately assess your strengths and weaknesses, and set ultimate and intermediate goals for both skills and racing. If you do this in conjunction with a training plan, everything is a whole lot easier. The next order of business is to determine which skills you want to develop and in what order. It's easy to get carried away with all this planning and forget that you have a life. So, be realistic about the amount of time you have for all this training. Once you've figured out your overall time frame, goals, and weaknesses and strengths, you can start breaking your training plan down into six-week blocks. Now you've really got a jump on the rest of the field. Still, you might want to read on to Chapter 9, and get the full rundown on the essentials of cross-country riding techniques. It's the kind of stuff that comes in real handy in a race.

NOTES ON WEIGHT TRAINING

The spread of sessions over a week

If three workouts a week: Monday, Wednesday, Friday.

If four workouts a week: Monday, Tuesday, rest on Wednesday, and workout again on Thursday, Friday.

Weightlifting when traveling

When traveling, it's not always easy to find a gym where you can lift. So, it's a good idea to plan out a maintenance workout that uses the resistance of your own body mass. Push-ups (by varying your hand position you can emphasize different muscle groups), push-ups with your feet on the back of a chair, sit-ups, back raises, triceps presses (using one or two chairs), pull-ups, and hand-stand push-ups make a pretty good upper-body workout. For your legs, the one-legged squat is hard to beat for strength and balance. (To do this exercise, hold one leg in front of you, while you squat with the other.) This whole maintenance workout will take you less than half an hour. Make sure that you don't overcompensate for the lack of your usual workout by going ballistic on pull-ups and wake up so sore the next morning that you can barely move your arms.

Chapter 9

Cross-country riding skills

Rolling resistance and gravity are the main forces to overcome in cross-country mountain biking. (The average speed of a typical World Cup race is between 12 and 15 mph, which means aerodynamic considerations are relatively minor.) So, the way you handle rough terrain and obstacles can make the difference between placing first or finishing in the middle of the pack. Every time you miss the perfect line or lose control on a corner, your competitors gain an advantage and you lose valuable seconds. As for descending, the less-skilled rider can lose up to a minute on a one-mile descent — and that's without crashing. When you consider how slim the margin is that separates the winner of a cross-country race from the second-place finisher, a minute is a long, long time. I've even seen this kind of separation happen at the World Cup level.

In order to be successful at cross-country racing, you must stay relaxed while constantly looking ahead, reading the terrain for every little section that offers you a small advantage. The overall effect of this relaxed vigilance is that your bike rolls over the ground at a greater speed with less effort.

In this chapter, Henk — who has earned a reputation for being one of the smoothest, most accomplished riders on the pro circuit — demonstrates some of the skills and knowledge that can help you glide over the terrain, instead of wrestling with it.

According to Henk: "Smoothness on a bike is partly a gift from nature, but everyone can improve their style. One thing you have to do is train on different loops. You must learn to choose lines on unfamiliar tracks. Try to go out and find new places

9.1 THE WIDE LINE.
Here Henk takes the long way around. He has spotted a smooth line of dirt on the outer rim of a rocky corner. The route he has chosen is a lot longer than the inside line, but by taking it he travels faster. The extra speed more than compensates for the additional distance traveled, and Henk exits the turn without the need to accelerate sharply. He also reaps the benefit of avoiding the jarring ride over the rocks.

with difficult sections. When I was learning cyclo-cross racing, I always changed the course I trained on. I always tried to find a course that made me ride over obstacles when I was already tired. When you are fresh you can ride a lot more things than when you are tired."

THE LINE

Most pros agree that "the line is everything." Classical rules of cornering (adapted from road cycling) don't always apply off-road. What may be the best line according to the laws of physics is often relegated to second or third choice due to the surface condition of the trail. Terrain almost always dictates the best line. This is illustrated clearly in Figure 9.1.

Henk says: "Line is really important. Sometimes you might be able to go very fast in one part of single-track, then suddenly you can't find the right line for the next part. For this reason, it's always better to hold back a little bit, give yourself more time to react to something unexpected, and stay smooth all the time."

Line on climbs

Nowhere on a cross-country course is your line more important than on technical climbs. Whether or not you are strong enough to make it to the top without a dismount is often immaterial — the real question is, can you stay balanced? In Figures 9.2-6 Henk shows how picking the right line helps you stay upright, while plenty of power comes from your legs. Another important factor in successfully riding up technical ascents is a smooth pedaling rhythm. While photographing this sequence, Henk put a foot down four times in a row on the step at the top, then something clicked, and he cleaned it the following eight times. Watching him as he mastered this maneuver, you could see that he had everything figured out — balance, right line, gears, pedal cadence, body position and weight shifts — he had it all put together in his mind. After that, he didn't have to think about it. He just did it.

9.2 *Rather than ride on the flat section of the track over the rocks, Henk climbs up on the smoother bank beside it. This line offers better pedaling rhythm and balance.*

9.3 *Henk's task now is to set himself up for the step ahead. He spots his entry channel.*

9.4 *A powerful pedal stroke is necessary here to give Henk the momentum to hop the back wheel over this protruding step. He is aiming for the small notch on the uphill side of the track.*

9.5 *At one point, he will need to make a strong upward thrust from the legs and hips if he is going to get the back wheel over the step, but he must position himself carefully for this. If his balance is too far to his left, his front wheel will wash out on the steep banking.*

9.6 *He moves his upper body slightly to the right of center and springs up. Although his back wheel must now travel over the protruding part of the step, this is not a problem because the front wheel has a clear rolling path ahead. He steers the front wheel so it comes under the center of his body, and he will pedal away having "cleaned" the step. Note that he has come forward to unweight his rear wheel.*

Steep climbs, loose surface

On some climbs, the challenge is to find a line that allows you to keep your balance; on others, the challenge is to keep the back wheel gripping and the front wheel steering. Figure 9.9 gives an example of this situation on a steep climb with a loose surface. On a climb such as this one, Henk's advice is to "steer with the whole body, not just with the knees and hips. Sometimes you can get a bit of extra leverage or balance from a knee or an elbow. Balance, strength, the right line are the keys to a climb like this. You also need to stay relaxed and flexible on steep climbs. If you are already tired at the start of the climb, for sure you are going to make some mistakes."

One of the most important points to remember about climb-

9.7 LOOSE CLIMB

The ground is covered with about two inches of fine, dry gravel. The corner curves to Henk's right. Steering is made more difficult because the gradient is very steep, and Henk must pull back on his handlebars to get pedaling leverage. This makes the front end lighter, which reduces steering control. To counter this, he gets his shoulders forward and down, but he is very careful to keep enough weight over the back wheel to ensure that the tire continues to grip on the loose surface. This he does by remaining seated, which pushes the wheel into the ground. When a surface is this loose, he cannot stand up on the pedals.

There is not one key, but several to riding hills of this nature. Yet whatever else Henk does, his pedaling effort must be smooth. Any jerky movements will make the wheel spin, and he will have to put a foot down. He has chosen a gear using the middle chainring and the largest rear cog. To ride a hill as steep as this in the middle ring without standing up requires great leg strength.

On a climb where steering was not as critical, Henk would sit farther back on his seat.

9.8, 9.9 *The rocky line does not look particularly challenging, but it's not worth risking a puncture for the thrill of a few bumps. Besides, it takes extra effort to handle the bumps, and cross-country racing is about conserving energy until the right opportunity emerges.*

ing is pacing yourself. Most riders slow down when they see the top approaching; they decide that their work is done and it's time for a well-earned rest. Make no mistake about it, this is a recipe for failure. The only way for a winning racer to crest a hill is by increasing the effort slightly as the hill starts to level off. This final effort doesn't need to last long, perhaps 50 or 100 yards into the descent, or plateau, if the climb leads to that. This is not only good for your mental toughness, but it also inflicts heavy damage on your opponent's morale.

Line on the descent

Riding back down the same stepped climb, Henk shows that the best line up can also be the best line down (Figs. 9.7 -8). This makes a lot of sense considering that the easiest way up should also be the best way down. Although the descent is not particularly challenging, he took care to avoid the loose volcanic stones lining the trail.

CORNERING

After the general advice given in Chapter 2, cornering is largely a matter of practice and something you have to get straight in your mind. Figures 9.10-12, on the following page, show Henk on the same corner used in the pictures illustrating intermittent braking in Chapter 2. Even though it has a steep gradient, is off-camber, and the surface is loose, Henk is taking the corner at racing speed.

In the two-picture sequence of Figures 9.13-14, on the following page, Henk is on a corner with a worse camber but a better surface. As in the earlier sequence, he shows exemplary control. His primary concern is to remain balanced on the bike, which he does without any superfluous movement. His comments about the corner: "Riding it now was not too difficult, but it would be harder in a race. You have to deal with fatigue then, and that makes everything more difficult.

"The inside line is a lot easier because you can ride on the slight berm (about two-inches high) near the center of the track (we made Henk take the outside line).

"The outside line is more difficult, but it's not super-technical. Weight should go on the rear wheel, use both brakes,

9.10-12 *Henk's weight bias is toward the rear of the bike. He is braking more with his rear brake than the front, although as the levers clearly show he uses both brakes throughout. The third picture in the sequence shows his rear wheel throwing up some gravel as he increases the braking pressure. His pedals remain at the horizontal position, and his knees and elbows are slightly flexed throughout.*

9.13-14 (OPPOSITE PAGE) *Using the outside line to avoid the pitch of this off-camber turn, Henk displays his world-championship form at top speed.*

9.15 *Entering the corner, Henk's shoulders are leading the way and his eyes are focused a few meters ahead, where he expects to make the next part of the turn. A finger rests on each brake lever in case he needs to suddenly reduce speed. His outside leg is down, and he's using it to help steer the bike. It's not apparent until the final picture, but the bike is leaning farther over than Henk's body. Henk's style of riding differs from Missy's in this way: He does not articulate at the waist to nearly the same extent that she does.*

9.16 *Hitting the apex of the corner, Henk's outside leg remains down and the inward rotation of it can be more clearly seen, with his knee pushed in close to the top tube. He is steering the bike with his hips, knees and shoulders.*

9.17 *The critical point passed, he now resumes pedaling, although his outside knee is still rotated inwards, helping the bike complete its turn.*

9.12

9.13

9.14

9.17

and keep your balance on the bike. If I carry too much speed through this, my front wheel will disappear."

The third sequence of pictures, in Figures 9.15-17, shows Henk on a faster corner, where he's attacking more. The surface is still not ideal: It's soft, and he has to take care that the front wheel doesn't wash out. He tries to prevent this by getting forward and low over the handlebars.

9.18-9.21 RIDING GULLIES
9.18 *Henk drops in with his weight pushed well back. At this point, he's already preparing for a sudden pull upward on the handlebars to get the front wheel moving up the sudden incline on the other side.*
9.19 *With the front wheel out of trouble, he now springs with his legs to help the rear wheel out of the gully. His weight has started to go forward, which relieves the pressure on the rear wheel.*

RIDING GULLIES

Sharp gullies can quickly separate rider from bike if you don't use the correct technique. In this situation, a rapid fore-aft weight shift is combined with a strong pull on the handlebars to keep the wheels rolling. If the timing is wrong, expect to fly over the bars and leave your bike in the ditch behind you. In Figures 9.18-21 Henk shows how it's done.

RUNNING GULLIES

Some gullies and other obstacles just can't be ridden — at least not quickly. In this case, the only option is to dismount and run. There are no hard-and-fast rules about when to dismount. Just make sure to do it before losing all your momentum, and hit the ground running.

According to Henk, "Things always change. You might have been able to ride a hill in training, when you were fresh, but when you are tired some things take more energy to ride because you make more mistakes and have to correct them. Even so, it is always best to decide in advance if you are going to ride it or dismount."

In order to dismount efficiently, you have to know how far from the obstacle to get off. If you dismount too early, you'll be passed by other riders. But if you leave it too late, you'll collide with the obstacle. So you have to get the feel of this for yourself. The technique Henk demonstrates in Figures 9.22-33 allows you to dismount right at the last second without hitting the obstacle. Further cross-country skills are illustrated in Chapter 15.

The following two chapters relate to downhill riding. Although these chapters do not contain a wealth of information for cross-country riders, they do contain useful snippets, so I encourage you to glance over them anyway, gleaning what you can. The next chapter of vital interest to cross-country riders is Chapter 12, **Winning the Inner Game.**

9.22-9.33 RUNNING GULLIES
9.22 *Henk is still braking as he starts his dismount. Notice how his right foot just barely clears the rear wheel.*
9.23 *Still under brakes, Henk prepares to pass his right leg in between his left leg and the bike frame. This will mean he can literally land running.*
9.24 *He has now slowed down enough so that he no longer needs his fingers on the brake levers.*
9.25 *He has taken the top tube of the bike with his right hand even before removing his left foot from the pedal. He removes his foot with a deft sideways movement.*
9.27 *Keeping his left hand on the handgrip, he prepares to leap over the gully.*
9.28 *As he leaps, he tries to keep the bike level to the ground on either side of the gully, or at least not let it fall beneath the level of the landing side. If it did, he would then have to use extra energy to lift it up again to the landing side.*
9.29-9.30 *As soon as possible, Henk starts preparing for the remount. He can do this as soon as he has both hands on the bars.*
9.31 *Henk dismounts by stepping with his left foot and throwing the right foot inches above the rear wheel. Henk can place a lot of weight on his arms at this point. His eyes are focused on the track ahead, checking that his path is clear.*
9.32-33 *Both feet go to meet the pedals. Henk has already made a mental note of the position in which he left them, so he doesn't need to take his eyes off the track to search for them. He clips in at about the same time that he starts pedaling, and he is away*

9.20 *His weight continues to push forward and he resumes pedaling.*
9.21 *Safely out, he can now return to the seated position and continue to ride away.*

This was not at all a comfortable-looking exercise. The reaction forces created by the sudden deceleration of the front wheel are considerable. The difficulty of then getting the rear wheel to bite into the soft ground, not just spin, is also apparent as Henk almost hops it out over the initial step.

C h a p t e r 1 0

The downhill year

This chapter is similar to Chapter 8, "The Cross-Country Year." However, the most salient parts — the training plan templates and training advice — are quite different. These two chapters are written this way on the supposition that few readers will choose to specialize in both cross-country and downhill.

To begin with, downhill racing is not a sprint event. Specifically, downhill racing is a "short endurance" race, comparable in character to the 3000 meter steeple-chase track event. The steeple-chase is a hellish hard race. I've trained for it, and believe me it is murder. Just like the steeple chase, downhill racers have to be very fit to maintain a near maximal heart rate for four to six minutes. I remember John Tomac once commenting after a downhill race in June," 192 (beats per minute), that's the highest it's been all season." But what makes the downhill super-tough is that you have to remain highly coordinated throughout the race or you'll end up with a mouth full of dirt ... or worse.

A British sports scientist, Chris Barnes, of Teeside University, studied a group of elite level British downhillers during a six-race series. He observed that the winners were riding at 95-percent of their maximum heart rate, whereas those who crashed were closer to the 100-percent mark. He noted that throughout the season all of the riders became more tolerant to blood lactate. Both of these observations indicate that a program of hard physical training will increase your chances of doing well in downhill competition.

Whether or not you choose to take this advice and follow a program of intensive physical training (sometimes referred to

as "pain"), you need a training plan. An annual training plan provides direction and focus as you first approach and then progress through the season. Training without a plan is a sure-fire formula for under-achievement. You would be amazed at how much more you learn about your own skills and abilities just by devising a training plan. Without question, one of these puppies is a must for every serious mountain bike racer.

Since it plays such an integral role in your day-to-day activities, putting together a training plan is a huge job. One that requires all of the dining room table, most of the day, several cups of coffee, and lengthy consultations with your partner and other family members about work/school schedules, weekends, birthdays, anniversaries and vacation time. Oh, and by the way, you will almost certainly need a crystal ball.

Seriously though, it is both inspirational and useful to make educated guesses about what you might be doing months in advance, particularly when it comes to deciding on the week when you want to have your best form of the year. Unfortunately, life has this way of trashing your best-laid plans in one fell swoop (then changes everything back two weeks later). In view of this, long-term plans should be drawn up as general guidelines. So you may ask, "Why bother creating such a detailed chart at all?" The answer is that it gives you something to shoot for; a plan for the future. A training plan is a non-linear chart that is built on blocks of time approximately six-weeks long. Like any map, it helps you get from where you are to where you want to be. If you are looking for a template for your first attempt at a training plan, try Diagram 7.2 in Chapter 7, instead of the super-detailed training plan in

Diagram 8.1. Clearly, the first draft of your training plan does not need the level of complexity in the later figure.

It is the purpose of this book to provide you with the knowledge you need for monitoring your own progress and grasping the basic principles of training. With practice, you should be able to recognize what your body is telling you: Whether the training is too much or not enough; and most importantly, how to avoid being carried off to the land of overtraining on the wings of enthusiasm.

The annual training overviews in Diagrams 10.1 and 10.2 lay out skeleton structures that have been tried and tested on a mixture of senior and junior riders. The unavoidable truth about any sensible training plan is that you must work out the details for yourself.

DETAILS YOU NEED TO WORK OUT FOR YOURSELF

• Your exact heart rates at the different levels of intensity.
• When you are ready to progress to a greater load (intensity) and volume (frequency) of training.
• Whether you want a training session to be, for example, a clinical set of repetitions on a hillside or an uplifting experience in The Great Outdoors, or a mixture of the two.
• How much time you can devote to training (I have suggested weekly hour totals that range from beginner-to-elite level competitors).

Please flip to appendix 7 (page 112) for Diagrams 10.1-10.2

NOTES ON THE SUGGESTED TRAINING PLANS

The following written training plans are not designed to be carried out to the letter. I have included them to give you an idea of the shape and sequence of training exercises. The pace of your training, and how much you increase it by, is something only you can decide.

The details given below take a keyhole view at particular periods. In the relevant period, you should make adjustments to the figures I have given, depending on the time of the period. In the earlier stages, you would expect to do a lighter volume, for example. In Diagram 10.2, I have made suggestions for varying the High Intensity Endurance (HIE) sessions.

If you are fit and healthy, then you should have no problems following the suggested programs. If you have any doubts about or problems with your health, consult a medical practitioner before you do any further planning.

GENERAL PREPARATION PHASE

Day of week/Training Aim	Exercise Options (Choose any one you like)
SUNDAY 3 hours LIE	MTB, road ride, xc ski, run, hike, aerobics
MONDAY 2 hours Cross Training 45 min Weights	MTB, downhill ski, snowboard, run, aerobics, gymnastics, basketball, martial arts
TUESDAY 45 min Weights	
WEDNESDAY 1 hour LIE	as above
THURSDAY 2 hours Cross Training 45 min Weights	as above
FRIDAY 45 min Weights	
SATURDAY	DAY OFF

NOTES

① Where a range of exercise options is listed alongside a long training session, you would be able to choose any combination of sessions.

For Cross Training sessions in this period, some riders enjoy a little motocross riding. If you can afford the equipment and can find a good venue, this type of cross training is about as good as it gets.

② Cross Training can be high-intensity exercise. The idea is to give yourself a good workout, and perhaps get a chance to train skills that can be transferred to mountain bike racing.

SPECIFIC PREPARATION PHASE

Day of week/Training Aim	Exercise Options
SUNDAY 1 hour HIE	on bicycle (if not possible, then on skis or running. If still not possible after two weeks, use a turbo trainer)
MONDAY 45 min REC	as above
TUESDAY 45 min AP	on a bicycle, either outside or on a turbo trainer
WEDNESDAY 30 min Lactate Tolerance	(this is the starting point. During this month you would build up by 10-15 minutes each session)
THURSDAY 1 hour HIE	as above
FRIDAY 1 hour HIE 30 min PCr	as above on a bicycle, either outdoors or a turbo trainer
SATURDAY	REST DAY

EARLY-SEASON COMPETITION

Day of week/Training Aim	Exercise Options
SUNDAY (*If not racing…*)	
1 hour HIE	pref. off-road
MONDAY 45 min REC	pref. on-road
TUESDAY 30 min Lactate Tolerance	
WEDNESDAY 45 min Aerobic Power	
THURSDAY 45 min REC	
FRIDAY 1.5 hour Fartlek	pref. on-road
45 min PCr	paying special attention
	to pedaling style
SATURDAY	DAY OFF

EASY WEEKS

You don't get a complete rest here, but it is a lull that some find a welcome and needed break for reasons of psychological refreshment as much as physiological recuperation.

You should do one session of High-Intensity Endurance for 1 hour, and one Fartlek session for 1-1.5 hours.

MAIN SEASON COMPETITION

Day of week/Training Aim	Exercise Options
SUNDAY RACE OR 1.5 hours HIE	pref. off-road
MONDAY 1 hour REC	pref. on-road
1 hour skills	
TUESDAY 1.5 hours HIE	pref. on-road
45 min Aerobic Power	off -road
WEDNESDAY 45 min REC	off-road
THURSDAY 45 min PCr	off-road
FRIDAY 1 hour skills training	off road
30 min LT	on-road
SATURDAY	DAY OFF

TRANSITION

The main purpose of this period is to relax and regenerate after the racing season. If you cannot bear the prospect of exercise, don't do any. But it is far better for you to do light exercise in this period than none at all. Do whatever you want to. This is the time to catch up on all those activities you used to love before you became addicted to mountain biking: kayaking or surfing — as long as the conditions aren't too heavy — running, in-line skating, basketball, volleyball, rock climbing, downhill skiing, ultimate Frisbee … you name it. The main thing is to relax, kick back and enjoy yourself. You've earned it.

GETTING DOWN TO PLANNING

When it comes to designing your program, there is no better time than now. If you are using this book to help you create your training plan, I suggest inserting a few book marks in the following chapters as you flip back and forth.

Chapter 4 outlined the training sessions, what each session does and how they should be approached. Chapter 5 introduced fitness testing protocols, therefore giving you a method of making adjustments to your training heart-rate zones as you get fitter. In Chapter 6, we looked at goal setting, and a way of analyzing your strengths and weaknesses with the intention of becoming a strong all-around rider. Then in Chapter 7, we saw that the training year is divided into periods of greater or lesser training loads, and how a path of gradual progression is created.

A really high-class training program combines the thoughts on training presented in these chapters into a comprehensive and reasoned plan for continuing improvement. The initial laying out of your plan might feel like a gigantic waste of time, but the knowledge that you have a solid training plan will give you confidence when race day comes around. And if you are considering making a change in your training, you can always go back and reference what you've done.

A training plan that really "clicks" with you, and that you feel completely at home with, can take years of fine-tuning. But no matter how much or little time it takes to get it right, there is no better time to start than right now.

STEP ONE — the backbone

This is your master plan. To get this set-up, return to Chapter 6 and follow the instructions. This gives you an idea of what you will be working on during several of your weekly sessions. Wherever you can, double up, so you train fitness and skills in one exercise.

STEP TWO — fitness

Make a rough fitness-training scheme along the same lines as Diagram 7.1. It is important to leave spaces so you can write in the skills you want to train in specific weeks or periods.

STEP THREE — riding and racing skills

Review your current situation analysis and fill in the skills you want to practice. This part should be planned no more than six weeks in advance, because it is heavily dependent on the rate at which you acquire new skills. Give priority to your weak points.

STEP FOUR - time allocation

Work out how much time you are going to have available,

and when you'll be involved with other things like work, school, vacations or travel assignments. Note the number of hours available in categories of days, weeks and months. Some of you may be fortunate enough to commute to work as part of your training effort.

STEP FIVE - putting it all together

This is where you start to fill in a chart similar to Diagrams 8.1-8.4. Use this page for your long-term goals, leaving short term goals and specific training sessions to be mapped out at a maximum of six weeks in advance.

So there you have it. Your annual training program has already taken shape. Look after it, and it will look after you. To help you progress smoothly through your season's training, here are a few notes of advice on day-to-day training.

NOTES ON FITNESS TRAINING

• If performing consecutive hard days, which you can do in cycling, work on different energy systems from one day to the next. Otherwise you risk overstressing a system. (see Chapter 3.)

• Avoid Overtraining. If you feel the approach of overtraining symptoms, or you are simply unable to complete the training sessions, alter your schedule so you can take a week off training altogether. In particular, reduce the volume of high-intensity sessions. One simple way to do this is by shifting to a 14-day cycle, instead of the seven-day programs I have outlined. After each day involving a repeat or fartlek session, do a day of Low Intensity Endurance or Recovery riding. For some riders, this might prove to be a more successful format right from the start, so be prepared to experiment. Just make sure to record everything in your *VeloNews* training diary.

• The pattern of training variations suggested in Diagrams 10.2 and 10.4 is only a suggestion. If you feel unready to step up a to a higher volume, don't try and keep up with the suggested schedule. Go at your own pace. Remember, I have no idea how you respond to training. This is one reason why it is always better to work with a good coach — one who can monitor your rate of progress, help balance your program and give you advice on a whole range of problem areas.

• If you are serious enough and experienced enough to train twice a day, here are some general guidelines:

① After your first session, put on dry clothes, eat, hydrate, shower, rest (get a massage if possible) — in that order. After the second session, you might want to shower first, but if you are training as hard as this, the sooner you can eat after exer-

cise the faster your recovery will be.

② Normally you won't do two hard sessions in one day. If you do, make one of them relatively brief, such as creatine phosphate and lactate tolerance training. (If you mix lactate tolerance with another type of training in a day, do the lactate-tolerance work last.)

③ During the race season, try not to fully deplete your glycogen stores in training. Once a week is more than enough exposure to glycogen depletion, and this will likely happen in a race anyway. If you do deplete your glycogen stores four or five days before a race and continue hard training in the following days, they will possibly be less than 100- percent come race day. While this is not necessarily a bad thing if done with care dur-

NOTES ON WEIGHT TRAINING

The spread of sessions over a week
If three workouts a week: Monday, Wednesday, Friday.
If four workouts a week: Monday, Tuesday, rest on Wednesday, and workout again on Thursday, Friday.

Weightlifting when traveling

When traveling, it's not always easy to find a gym where you can lift. So, it's a good idea to plan a maintenance workout that uses the resistance of your own body mass. Push-ups (by varying your hand position you can emphasize different muscle groups), push-ups with your feet on the back of a chair, sit-ups, back raises, triceps presses (using one or two chairs), pull-ups, and hand-stand push-ups make up a pretty good upper-body workout. For your legs, the one-legged squat is hard to beat for strength and balance. (To do this exercise, hold one leg in front of you, while you squat with the other.) This whole maintenance workout will take you less than a half-hour. Make sure that you don't overcompensate for the lack of your usual workout, go ballistic on pull-ups and wake up the next morning so sore that you can barely move your arms.

ing periods of heavy build-up training, you should avoid deplet-ing your glycogen stores in the mid-to-late race season. In this period, high-intensity sessions of one hour are quite adequate as aerobic training, even for pro-level racing, and take less recovery than longer sessions.

SUMMARY

To put together an effective training schedule, it requires a lot of time and thought. In so doing, you must accurately assess your strengths and weaknesses, and set ultimate and interme-diate goals for both skills and racing. If you do this in con-junction with a training plan, everything is a whole lot easier. The next order of business is to determine which skills you want to develop and in what order. It's easy to get carried away with all this planning and forget that you have a life. So, be realis-tic about the amount of time you have for all this training. Once you've figured out your overall time frame, goals, and weaknesses and strengths, you can start breaking your training plan down into six-week blocks. Now you've really got a jump on the rest of the field. Still, you might want to read on to Chapter 9, and get the full rundown on the essentials of cross-country riding techniques. It's the kind of stuff that comes in real handy in a race.

Chapter 11

Downhill skills

Success in downhill racing is more difficult to analyze than success in cross-country — partly because top downhill riders have come from every kind of background imaginable, including downhill skiing, BMX racing, motocross racing, and road racing. What we do know about downhill racing is that in order to win, a rider must be in peak physical condition, have a very positive mental attitude and razor-sharp skills.

Fitness and the psychological approach to training are discussed in Chapters 3, 4, and 7. In this chapter, Missy Giove outlines some of the many skills you'll need at your command in order to downhill like the pros.

THE "LINE"

As in cross-country riding, the line is everything, and the

major factor in determining it is ground conditions. The best line is not necessarily the shortest, or the one that you would choose if the ground were smooth. With a good eye for the easiest line, you can get away with less well-developed skills in other areas. Photo sequence 11.1-3 shows Missy delaying a turn until ground until the trail is free of debris.

11.1 *Entering the corner, Missy is looking to drive the bike around a tight line. Her elbows and knees are flexed, and her hips and knees are turned into the corner. Her eyes are looking where she wants to go.*

11.2 *Rocks to her left make it unwise to turn on the tight line, despite the ample suspension of her race bike. The gap is ahead of her. She delays the turn by sitting up a little and moving her hips and knees back toward the center line of the bike.*

11.3 *(a) At the gap, she tilts the bike, and drives her hips and knees into the corner. (b) Missy gives the front wheel extra traction by putting her weight forward.*

The next sequence of photos, Figures 11.4-6, also deal with lines through rough terrain. Here, Missy puts a foot out as she goes through the critical part of the corner, and although the ground is possibly rougher at the exit than through the corner, she is sufficiently stable at that point to bring her inside foot back to the pedal. This is where she will need it, in order to sprint out of the turn onto the straight.

We continue our study of good lines in Figures 11.7-10. Here, Missy sweeps around an awkward, off-camber corner. Figure 11.11 shows Missy coming out of a very steep descent onto an off-camber transition. She doesn't appear too flustered here, and perhaps that's because she follows her own advice: "Regulate your speed, know how fast you can go into that turn. If you go in too fast, you'll go off the trail. So know your tires. Know how fast they can go before they break loose, and know how many feet they will slide before they hook-up (grip) again.

"On an off-camber turn, keep off your brakes — both front and rear. Brake before the turn, get balanced, then let your bike just slide through the turn and pedal out of it. The earlier you hook-up again the better, and sometimes if you can put half a pedal stroke in while braking, that will help your tires grip.

11.7 *Missy knows the corner well, so she knows how her approach will be. A rider unfamiliar with the terrain probably would have taken a tighter line, then gotten into trouble on the rocks strewn on the inside of the corner.*

11.8 *Although the tight line is preferable, Missy stays wide. She is heavily weighting the outside of the bike to keep her center of balance over the wheels. This helps the tires bite into the off-sloping surface.*

11.9 *This is where she gets the payback. Because she has taken a wider line through the corner, her exit line can be tighter. She needs a tighter line because it is a narrow track with a drop-off to the left. Notice how she continues to lean the bike heavily and place her weight to the outside.*

11.10 *Missy exits the corner onto a section of heavily off-cambered track. She keeps the bike turning on a gentle arc, and gradually it will climb back up the slope toward the center of the trail. When the camber of the trail offers so little for the tires, movements must be slow and deliberate. Anything hurried could easily lead to a wheel washing out.*

11.11 *She has resumed pedaling, but her position is still very much to the outside of the bike. This weights the inside edge of the tires, helping them to track when there is not much to prevent them from sliding away.*

"Your weight should be heavily on your outside foot, and you should countersteer. By that I mean steering your wheel in the opposite direction of the turn: On a right-hand turn, I would push with my right arm and pull back with my left arm. This puts more pressure on the front end and helps the front wheel to keep track." For more information on countersteering, see Chapter 2 under **Steering and Cornering**.

11.12 *Missy has exited the gully at speed and swung back out to prepare for the corner. In this frame, she has corrected her line, straightening up and aiming for a depression in between some car tire tracks.*

11.13 *She goes though a patch of loose dirt and briefly loses control of the front wheel, as the small spray of dirt at the right of the tire shows. To counter this, she gets over the handlebars and puts a foot out for extra stability. When she puts a foot out, her waist moves less.*

11.14 *Missy is back in full control, and her bike is cornering like it was on rails.*

Whether you are turning or not, the quickest way to psyche yourself out on a serious descent is to focus on the obstacles. The truth is that different types of terrain offer a variety of opportunities as well as problems. By learning how to pick up on the opportunities quickly — and to predict where the next one might be — you can get out of some nasty situations and pick up time on your competitors. For example, Missy finds a useful groove in Figures 11.12-14. Notice that in this sequence she puts out her inside foot. Missy gives her reasons why riders do this: "If you're coming into a corner real hot, and your bike's leaned over at an extreme angle, you could put your foot out to save yourself if you fall, and to give yourself a lower center of gravity, which places more weight on your tires. Some riders are more comfortable doing this, and there are some that hardly ever do. If you watch Nicolas Vouilloz on a downhill

run, he almost never puts a foot out. He has a great sense of balance and stays very centered over his bike."

When you are cornering or navigating around a major obstacle (deep puddle, large rock, loose terrain like sand or gravel), it might be easier to leave the trail for a second than slow down to crawling speed. Paris-Roubaix racers are famous for escaping the pavé and riding on the shoulder of the road. This same technique applies equally well to downhilling. Missy demonstrates her off-the-trail skills in Figures 11.15-19. Here she has seen a natural berm that offers a high-speed alternative to the main trail.

Figures 11.20-24 show Missy taking a wide line through a tight right-hand turn. As she powers away from the corner, it becomes clear why the wide line was her choice: A tighter line through the corner would have led to a wide exit line, which would have put her into the weeds.

11.15 *Missy heads off the trail.*
11.16 *Her intention is to use the bank to her right as a berm. She is leaning the bike slightly to the right at this stage.*
11.17 *The soil of the bank is soft, and as she unweights the bike — which she must do to change the lean from left to right — there is a small amount of front-wheel washout, evidenced by the dirt spray from the tire.*
11.18 *Missy now has the bike leaning to the left, and she is starting to bring the back wheel around to prepare to exit the berm. She does this by applying the back brake.*
11.19 *She gets forward a little, allowing the rear wheel to break free. With her weight still pushing down to the left of the wheel, there is only one direction for it to go: to the right, which it does with a big shower of dirt. She is soon perfectly lined up to exit the corner.*

11.20-11.24 TAKING THE WIDE LINE

11.20 *Entering the corner, Missy has decided on a wide line. As she approaches, she is already looking ahead at where she needs to be to set up her exit. Notice how her position is more upright on the bike. She has raised herself slightly out of the seat and her shoulders are relatively high above the handlebars. This is because she is unweighting, to change the tilt of the bike from left to right.*

11.21 *She gets the bike leaning to the right, and steers it around with her knees, hips and shoulders. She comes down slightly over the handlebars to push*

the front wheel into the ground, and by so doing, adds to her stability.

11.22 *The wide line not only gives her a nice natural berm, but it also sets her into a nice groove in the track.*

11.23 *She hits the back brake to set the bike properly for the exit.*

11.24 *As she exits the turn, Missy's choice of lines makes even more sense. Only the wide line offers a tight enough exit on this single-track bend. As can be seen by the set of her knees and hips, Missy continues to steer toward the center of the track as she completes her exit.*

11.25-27 SMALL BERM AND TIGHT CORNER

11.25 *We pick up the sequence with Missy in a classic stance: The bike is tilted and she is leaning to the outside of the corner. At this point, she has put her inside foot down and forward and is pushing the front wheel into the dirt. Her aim is to get the back wheel loose and come around quickly. To* assist this, she pulls sharply on the rear brake.

11.26 *The wheel has come around, and she relaxes the rear brake. Her left foot starts to move back to the pedal...*

11.27 *...and she sprints away from the corner.*

11.28-11.31 HOW TO RIDE A BERM

11.28 *Missy steadies herself as she hits the banking. Her right arm is going up, and she has already unweighted the bike, ready to tilt it and push the tires down into the ground for extra traction. Note that she has her pedals in a horizontal position, with the outer pedal forward. This helps her hip-and-knee action.*

11.29 *This is the critical part of the corner, where a lot of riders lose it. Missy has a lot of weight over the front wheel. Her right elbow is high as she cranks the bike over. Wide handlebars help a lot at times like this. Her outer knee and hip are pushing to the inside of the corner. Her vision is a few meters ahead of the bike.*

11.30 *She starts to straighten up and prepare for the exit. By this point, she is ready to start pedaling. She no longer needs her outer pedal in the forward position to aid the turn.*

11.31 *Missy continues to sprint out of the turn.*

Riding berms

Berms can provide very fast, wide lines around corners, provided that the front wheel doesn't wash out. Fortunately, this is relatively easy to prevent. If you stay low, slow yourself down with the front brake and put the right amount of weight on the front wheel *before* going into the turn, you should be fine. Missy demonstrates the proper technique on a small berm in Figures 11.25-27. This technique also works well on tight corners.

In the sequence in Figures 11.28-31, Missy hits a berm in full flight. Notice that she doesn't start pedaling until she has passed the critical point and the bike is starting to exit the turn.

Lifting the front wheel

The problem of raising the front wheel while going down a steep slope has had a major effect on the design of downhill bikes, primarily their high handlebar position. Note that I didn't say "picking up" the front wheel. You don't pick it up; even Arnold Schwartzenegger's arms aren't that strong. The way to raise the front end is to lean back with your back and shoulders and more or less guide the front into the air with your arms and hands. In Figure 11.32, Missy shows how it's done. The drop-off that she's going over is big enough to require her to keep her front end up, or risk doing a face plant over the handlebars.

11.32 *When you are plummeting down a steep descent, it is not always easy to find the time and space to get your weight back on the bike and raise the front wheel. When you see drops like this one, you realize why it's worth practicing this skill. Here, Missy jumps a ledge that would probably throw her over the bars if she attempted to ride down it. To prepare, she has put her butt behind the seat, pushed against the pedals and pulled up on the handlebars. Notice that she is not using the brakes. Sometimes in situations like this it is better to let the bike roll and pick up momentum, then deal with the speed when you come to an easier section of track. Of course, you could only take such an approach if you were absolutely certain of what lay ahead.*

Single-track

The final sequence in this chapter, Figures 11.33-38, illustrates the rhythm and flow of single-track downhilling. Readers who have a background in downhill skiing might notice certain parallels, particularly in the way Missy steers with her hips and knees, and shifts her weight from left foot to right. Like many pro downhill racers, she's absolutely convinced about the transferability of skills from one sport to the other: "There are a lot of parallels with the way downhill skiing and mountain biking feel. This whole centerline thing, that feels the same. You try and keep your shoulders square while the bottom half turns; you push the inside arm down and forward, so much of the turning force comes from the way you point your hips and knees. The two actions are different in some ways, but they really have a lot in common."

If you have not read Chapter 2, I suggest you take a look at the **Steering and Cornering** section. This section may provide you with some insight into how to corner with more rhythm and control.

Common mistakes

Before leaving this chapter, I'll relay some advice from Missy about common mistakes: "The main mistake I see people make with mountain biking, period, is that they're too stiff. People would ride a lot better if they were relaxed.

"Another mistake is that people ride sitting down. It's a simple mistake. You can't control your bike sitting down, you have to stand up to control it, for the most part. There may be sections where you can sit and hammer, but even then you're not actually placing all your weight on your seat.

"Hitting the front brake at the apex of a turn is definitely going to cause your front wheel to wash out. You should brake early, set up, let go of the brakes — maybe drag your rear brake depending on what type of turn it is. But don't hit the front brake in the middle of a turn, right when you're leaning your bike over.

"All top downhillers train differently. That's individual. Our training programs have most of the same components, only in different proportions. But the one thing that every top rider has in common is that they all train hard. Hard work is the key."

Now that you've seen some of the basic skills utilized by successful downhill racers, it's up to you to go out and practice them. Be forewarned that it will take many hours to make substantial progress, and you'll almost certainly feel fed up and frustrated several times while waiting for a breakthrough. To help you, the next chapter covers an enlightened approach to learning skills — not only for downhill racing but for life itself.

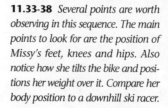

11.33-38 *Several points are worth observing in this sequence. The main points to look for are the position of Missy's feet, knees and hips. Also notice how she tilts the bike and positions her weight over it. Compare her body position to a downhill ski racer.*

Chapter 12

Winning the Inner Game

THE INNER GAME APPROACH TO SKILLS

I sometimes think about packing in the journalism business and going back to school to get an advanced graduate degree in sports psychology. I can see it now: I'd develop a revolutionary mental approach to mountain bike training and racing, and become rich, famous and universally praised. Actually, a tennis pro named W. Timothy Gallwey did just that. He devised something called the Inner Game, which is a way of thinking about competitive sports that makes it much easier to learn and perform to the best of your ability.

I haven't seen, nor can I think of, a better approach than Gallwey's to the mental skills you'll need to make big improvements as a mountain biker. I recommend Gallwey's book, *The Inner Game of Tennis*. It has less to do with tennis and more to do with the way we view ourselves and the sports we compete in, and it will expand on many of the points I make in this chapter. So read it. One of the most effective lecturers and sports teachers I had at the University of Loughborough incorporated Gallwey's work into his course plan. Much of the material in this chapter is inspired by Gallwey's work.

Understanding how the Inner Game affects mountain bike riding can be a huge help with your technical skills, as well as overcoming the mental obstacles that prevent you from becoming the rider you want to be. The four basic skills of the Inner Game approach are:

① Letting go of judgments
② The art of programming with images
③ Letting it happen
④ Concentration

In this chapter, I have adopted these elements from Gallwey and put them into the context of mountain bike riding and racing.

THE TWO SELVES

Have you ever given yourself verbal coaching or advice when on a mountain bike? You know, things like, "Pull back and up on those pedals," or "Get more weight on that front wheel." And then have you praised or chastised yourself, according to the outcome? I think most riders do this to some degree. I certainly have. This is what Gallwey calls "Self One talking to Self Two." Self One is the conscious, managing part of the mind that is linked to the cognitive parts of the brain; it gives the instructions. Self Two is the subconscious mind, the part linked to the central nervous system, which fires off the signals making your muscles contract and relax. Self Two hears everything, forgets nothing and is far from stupid. After pulling one wheelie, Self Two knows forever which muscles to contract and relax in order to perform this skill.

Self One tends to get in the way when it comes to performing skills. Look at the faces of many riders on a descent: twisted and contorted, anxious, worrying about crashing, the rider behind them, the crowd, or any number of things. If these riders could only find a way to harness all the energy they put into a grimace... Unfortunately, the face muscles don't push the pedals, nor spring the bike off the ground, nor do they help concentration. They do, however, indicate that Self One is interfering with the work of Self Two. The intellectual Self One — which is supposed to be offering reasoned, tactical decisions about the best line and speed, or when to push out some super-hard pedal strokes — has a tendency to show a lack of trust in Self Two.

The Inner Game of mountain biking requires that Self One lets Self Two get on with its job. The best way to achieve this state of inner calm is by letting go of judgments about your performance. Thinking too much or trying too hard spoils the effort. Just let it happen. Look at it this way, you do not try to orchestrate the movement of your hand to your mouth when eating. Your hand has been there before and knows exactly how to get there. You don't have to think about it. The same is true of a bunny hop, or a wheelie, or sliding around a turn without out using your brakes. Sure, these movements are more complicated, but the principle is the same. Just because you're in a race, Self Two hasn't forgotten how to bunny hop a rock — something you've practiced over-and-over when you're just riding around — but when Self-One starts giving commands like "pull up now," you only clog your mind with a lot of extra chatter, instead of freeing up space for tactical decisions. As you can see, Self-One talk is extremely counter productive.

If you make a mistake and misjudge a turn, you'll immediately know not to do it that way again. Certainly, it's worth making an assessment of how you handled a difficult hairpin, or hopped a log, but there's a way to do this without falling into the trap of labeling your performance "good" or "bad."

Whether the problem is that you're having trouble getting your front wheel high enough to clear a step, or you're persistently mistiming a pre-jump, the solution is the same. Save your judgments for the moral decisions in your life — we all have enough of those to go around — and free-up the autonomic part of your mind. You can't be "bad" because you haven't learned to pull a wheelie. All you can be is unskilled at wheelies. Remember: a wheelie is a skill, and skills can be learned. All you need to know is what to do and how it feels. Perhaps nobody, including yourself, has yet been able to give you the required information in a way that you can digest — more on that later on in this chapter.

Self One might be called the ego-mind. Harmony between the two selves is achieved when the mind is quiet. This kind of inner harmony is necessary to produce peak performance. In a peak state, or flow, or zone, or whatever else you want to call it, you can expect to feel egoless. That is, you just perceive what is required and act according to the demands of the situation. Often, this feels effortless. You don't feel like you want, or hope, or fear, or demand anything, you just let it happen. For some, this is a spiritual experience. You have the inner assurance that the section can be ridden without trying to do it. Sure, it will take some effort, but that effort is readily there in the right quantities, supplied subconsciously by Self Two, and not forced in any way.

I remember a friend and I were sitting on a log in the Australian Alps one spring day a few years back. Magpies were flying helter-skelter through a small thicket of sapling poplar trees that had not yet grown their summer foliage. Despite flying remarkably quickly through this intricate obstacle course, the birds never once hit a tree. "That just proves they don't have egos," commented my friend. "Why?" I asked. "Because if you don't have an ego, you don't doubt yourself, and most crashes (suddenly he was referring to skiing) happen when self-doubt creeps in," he answered. The same applies to mountain biking.

STEPS TO QUIETING THE MIND

Letting go of a judgment about a performance as "good" or "bad" is a major step toward a quiet mind — one in which Self One isn't constantly talking to you. Let's say you clear a tabletop jump, skim over a big washboard, or hit a berm hard and true: You ain't got time to congratulate yourself, so don't bother trying. Also, if you decide it was "good," you'll put pressure on yourself to repeat it. On the other hand, if you get it wrong, you'll only interfere with the task at hand if you start thinking about what went wrong and how you could and should have done it better.

All this leads to constant evaluation and self-conscious performance. It also leads to generalizations, like "I'm no good at riding berms," which become self-fulfilling prophecies. The least you can do to help is give yourself every opportunity to excel. Being uncritical doesn't mean that you should ignore errors; it just means that you don't think about them while you're riding. After a race or ride, you can quantify your errors and rate your performance any way you want to, and *then* you can seek out the causes. If you can divorce yourself from judgment and ego reactions during the ride, you'll be well on your way to minimal interference.

STAYING LOOSE

"You can't afford to waste any energy out there," says Henk Djernis. This advice applies to downhill racing as well as cross-country. The following section is linked to this point.

Think for a second about the way body movement works. One group of muscles contract to pull the limb one way while another relaxes, then the first group relaxes while the second group contracts to pull the limb back again. When fear, uncertainty or self-consciousness enters into this complex act of coordinated impulses, the nerve signals can get jammed and muscles have a tendency to lock-up. That is, an antagonistic pair of muscles (biceps and triceps, for example) contract against each other. The result is what is commonly referred to as "freezing up." Under these conditions, displaying any sort of skill is next to impossible.

Fear can be dealt with by practicing on low-risk obstacles. Uncertainty? Try emulating or caricaturing a famous rider; the idea here is to take your mind off your own self talk — provided that you don't jump on your own case for not riding as well as the rider you are attempting to emulate. The potential plus of this exercise is that you might accidentally stumble across a useful riding technique. As for self-consciousness, that should gradually disappear as you become absorbed in the tasks at hand — a single-track mind.

LEARN FROM THE PROS

Go to any professional mountain bike race and watch the racers. Take a pad and make notes. When it's time for your next practice session, the notes will help you recall what you saw. Go to different parts of the course and get a feeling for the way each section is ridden. Observe in particular the body movements of the riders: knees, hips, shoulders, elbows, back and facial expressions. You'll see that on some obstacles, many different styles are used, and for other obstacles the same style is adopted by almost all riders. As you learn new skills, try and replicate some of these movements and see what happens. For some comic relief, try replicating the facial expressions in particular.

This may sound like a frivolous exercise, but self-doubt can be expelled with remarkable ease. You'll need your notes about how the pros ride for the next exercise also.

Looking good on the bike

Here you have to imagine you are your favorite rider. It should be really easy if you want to emulate Henk or Missy, because there are so many pictures of them in this book. Try and assume the same postures. Feel like a fool? Don't, you look like a pro! And remember, even the pros don't get it right every time.

When Henk was demonstrating skills for some of these photos, there was one maneuver he got wrong time and time again. He kept on riding back over the same obstacle, trying to find the solution. His approach was that of one who has mastered the Inner Game: there was never a hint of frustration or self-criticism. All he said was, "It's really funny, I didn't have any problems on this yesterday. I just can't quite remem-

ber what I was doing." There were no self-recriminations, just a genuine curiosity that there was more to riding this section than he had at first believed. Then a few attempts later it clicked. There was no obvious self-congratulation, just satisfaction at having solved the problem, and he didn't get it wrong thereafter.

Something else that will help is to practice the facial expressions of the pros. Wear them when you're riding, for they have a remarkable influence on your state of mind. If in doubt, smile. This was my savior when learning to juggle. Anytime I started to get frustrated, I'd put on a happy, flexible — not fixed — smile, and within seconds the balls would be flowing rhythmically again.

DEVELOPING YOUR STYLE

If you look at the styles of riders, there are a few distinct models. Henk and Missy are almost opposites. Missy, with her expressive, big movements, is closer to the style of John Tomac or Franck Roman than she is to Henk's contained, economical style, which is more akin to a rider like Regina Stiefl or Nicolas Vouilloz.

You might notice that I named six of the top riders of our day in the last sentence. Although the styles of the riders mentioned are more comparable to some than others, all look quite distinctive, and each has produced world championship results. You'll be able to identify your own style with one particular rider more than any other, but sometimes when practicing, try emulating the movements of a rider whose style looks nothing like yours. You can learn from this exercise, by making more exaggerated or more subdued movements than you would normally. In fact, you might even discover new facets of your own ability.

SKILL DEVELOPMENT

A new or improved skill is something that you learn by letting it unfold in you without interference, not by telling yourself what to do. Take the bunny hop, for example. Imagine how everything feels: the crouch, the spring, drawing the legs and arms up under you, the weightlessness of the bike, and then your limb extension again before landing and absorbing the impact with another crouch. If you have a clear idea of what you're looking for, you stand a much better chance of finding it.

When you see a giant of a man like Jake Watson hop a

mountain bike four feet into the air from a flat start, he makes it look very simple. If you asked him to describe how he does it, I have no doubt he would do so in simple terms. Yet if the task were thoroughly analyzed, it would yield a long list of dos and don'ts. Such in-depth analysis is less important than getting the basics right, and then probing around for the rest by experimenting and taking tips from your friends or, if you have one, a coach. If you tried to itemize every part of a bunny hop, you'd end up with a list that is too complex to do anything but confuse you.

If you have trouble, say, bunny-hopping a log, the Inner Game way of learning would have you try it something like this:

• Step one — Take an interested, yet detached look at what you're doing. For example, you may say to yourself, "My back wheel is crashing into the log, and I'm swerving to the left on landing. My friend tells me that I'm hardly compressing and springing with my legs; better check my arms also. He says I appear to pull up more forcefully with my right arm. Although on that second attempt, I actually felt the back wheel lift off the ground."

• Step two — Ask yourself to change your programming with image and feel. Don't use commands. You can show Self Two what you want to accomplish by imagining how it will look and feel. Also, if you want to, you can practice parts of the bunny-hop on their own, like how it feels to compress your lower body then bounce back up with a spring, bringing the pedals up with you, and how it feels to smoothly pull the handlebars in toward your chest. In this process, use as much imagination as you want, and be careful not to identify or correct errors.

• Step three — Let it happen. Now that you have given your body the program to perform, permit it the freedom to do so. This means no self-coaching; remember that Self One is not involved in this, you are now deep into the domain of Self Two. Effort is initiated by Self One, but nothing is forced. Self One just takes a step back and trusts Self Two to flow freely and smoothly.

• Step four — Interested, detached observation of the results, leading to continuing observation of the process until behavior is automatic. Although you know your objective, you have no emotional involvement in achieving it. Therefore, you're able to experience the results calmly, and feel what is happening to you and your bike. By doing so, you will achieve

your highest level of concentration and rapid learning. Reprogramming is only needed if the results don't conform to the image given. If the results are what was requested, simply continue to observe the ongoing evolution. Watch it change, but don't do the changing. Remember: Will power is good for getting you on your bike, but you can't will yourself to do a perfect bunny hop over a log. You have to be willing to give up control and trust that your subconscious mind already knows how to do it.

WAYS IN WHICH YOU CAN FALL BACK INTO BAD HABITS

This might have happened to you already: You've learned a new skill, or have raised your level in an existing skill, and you've made the mistake of telling yourself or your friends how good you are now. So then next time you go to do it, feeling you have something to live up to, you completely blow it.

Slipping into the Self Two state of mind comes readily with practice, yet Self One is always lurking close by, wanting to get involved and thereby interfering with your concentration. But that's just what Self One is like. Since it's the thinking, intellectual part of you, it's naturally interested in everything you do. To prevent Self One from interfering, it often helps to create a harmless diversion channel for it, enabling you to keep your attention focused on the task being carried out.

Diverting Self One involves focusing on something relevant, like the line you are going to take. This means shutting out extra stuff, like the spectators, or how close the rider behind you is, or what you wouldn't do for a nice cool drink. In order to stay focused on your line, you might want to notice the details of objects lying on it.

Now that you're starting to concentrate, the mechanical side of your actions will be happening without your realizing it. Other things exist that you can concentrate on. First is listening. Listening to the sound of your tires as they encounter different types of terrain is a great learning tool. How do they sound when you're braking, or sliding? Or slipping in mud? And at different speeds? This catalogue of sounds will gradually start helping Self Two do what's necessary for a range of different situations. When it comes to performing the braking, gear changing, leaning, lifting, hopping and all those other matters, you'll be focused and ready to deal with them.

Another essential part of concentration is feeling and rhythm. Be aware of certain feelings in the body as particular skills are

executed. For example, I look for the feeling of my quads working as I compress before a bunny-hop; I can feel my legs piv-
oting from my hips on down while my pelvis feels level. I'm
pedaling smoothly up a steep climb.

Develop a sense of rhythm by paying attention to the way
your body feels. Rhythm makes an enormous contribution to
a smooth and fluid style. It might be how long you delay a
pedal stroke as you pass over a step or as you enter a corner, or
switching your weight from outside to inside as you prepare to
get the back wheel moving sideways. As you become aware of
these rhythms and concentrate on them, their movement
becomes smoother and less hurried.

Particularly important is getting a fluid feeling for braking.
Notice how hard you pull on the brakes to create a small reduction in wheel speed, and how hard you pull when the wheel
locks up. It's also important to have a feeling for things like
body position. Know how it feels in the neutral position, or how
far the bike is leaning, and how far it can lean on different sur-
faces. Get the feel of the waist articulation as you go around a
corner, and how much weight to put on your outside foot as
you lean the bike into a turn.

In general, be aware of how your body feels in and out of
positions, and moving in between positions. But remember that
it becomes much harder to see or feel anything well if you are
thinking about how you should be moving.

SUMMARY

I assume that you're reading this book because you want to
learn more about mountain bike racing. Well, one thing that
you might consider is what you really want to have happen
when you're in a race. Do you want to win? Do you want to
do better than last time? Do you want to beat your friends or
fellow club members? All of these are quite valid desires to take
with you into a race. Making efficient use of your energy and
achieving your goals is what this chapter is all about. When
you learn to go beyond the negative self-talk of Self One, you'll
be surprised to find that your goals are much easier to attain.

Chapter 13

Nutrition for mountain bike racing

All athletes, including mountain bikers, are constantly looking for that special something that will raise them above the rest. As they hone their bodies through the process of training, they know that careful preparation and attention to detail will maximize their hard work. Since mountain-bike racing emerged in the late 1970s, the importance of nutrition in this process of fine-tuning has become increasingly evident. In fact, sports nutrition has become the modern panacea of the serious racer.

Nevertheless, despite a general acceptance of the importance of a well-balanced diet, the concept of optimal nutrition is not as clearly defined as some might think. In a quest for the winning edge, athletes are susceptible to commercially-driven fadism on the one hand, or folklore and myth on the other. It's important to emphasize at this point that optimal nutrition doesn't come in a bottle.

This chapter will help you avoid the pitfalls of marketing by examining sports nutrition from a performance perspective. It will address the key issues underpinning appropriate nutrition for mountain-bike racing, and examine how healthy, well-balanced eating can be incorporated into a lifestyle divided between family, work and training commitments.

BASIC NUTRITION

The message is very simple: A balanced diet for life provides the essential foundations for an optimal sports diet. The needs of an elite mountain biker are qualitatively the same as those of the average man or woman in the street; although quantitatively there may be a huge difference!

A healthy, well-balanced diet must contain the right amounts of essential nutrients. In terms of providing the body with fuel, carbohydrates and fats are the most important. Carbohydrates can be simply classified as sugars (simple carbohydrates providing an immediate burst of energy) or starches (complex carbohydrates releasing their energy over a longer period). Fruit, fruit juices, pastries and candies provide simple carbohydrates, whereas potatoes, brown rice, whole grain bread, pasta, oatmeal, beans and vegetables provide complex carbohydrates. A small amount of fat is also necessary in a balanced diet. As well as providing energy and acting as a medium allowing various micronutrients to be absorbed into the body, fat performs several essential structural and functional roles. Protein, made up of smaller units called amino acids, only covers a small fraction of the total energy demand, even under the most extreme circumstances. The main function of protein is concerned with growth and repair, providing the basic building blocks for any physiological training adaptations.

Other essential nutrients which must be provided by the daily diet include water, vitamins, minerals and fiber. Water performs a central structural role in the body (more than 60 percent of the body's mass is fluid), but it's also important in the circulatory system and in regulating body temperature. Vitamins are only required in very small amounts, but are essential in the regulation of various processes, and they must be contained in the diet on a daily basis. Similarly, minerals must be provided in the daily diet, as they are involved in a number of regulatory roles. In addition, minerals are involved in some of the body's general maintenance. For example, cal-

THE VEGETARIAN MOUNTAIN BIKER

There is no real nutritional reason why vegetarian mountain bikers should experience any disadvantages in comparison to their meat-eating counterparts; however, they do need to think more carefully about organizing their diet. Specifically, they have to watch their protein intake with respect to the range of amino acids.

Most of the amino acids we need can be manufactured in the body from other amino acids. However, there are eight essential amino acids that can only be obtained from the food we eat. Animal sources of protein (meats, fish, eggs, milk, yogurt and cheese) contain all the essential amino acids. In contrast, vegetable sources of protein may not contain all the required amino acids in one serving, meaning that vegetable foods need to be combined in order to ensure that the body receives all the essential amino acids on a daily basis.

It should be noted that some sources of vegetable proteins, such as soybeans and wheat germ, are better than others. It is a good idea to incorporate these higher quality proteins into your menu at some point during the course of the day — such as adding wheat germ to your breakfast cereal, or including a soybean products like tempeh or tofu in your main meal.

cium helps to strengthen bones, whereas iron is required for the manufacture of new red blood cells.

Finally, the diet must provide fiber, to smooth the passage of food along the digestive tract. A long-term deficiency in fiber, perhaps as a consequence of eating too many highly processed foods, has been associated with digestive problems such as constipation and gallstones.

FUELING THE BODY

As discussed in Chapter 3, exercising muscles are powered primarily by a mixture of carbohydrates and fats. Both the intensity and the duration of the exercise will determine which fuel is predominantly used.

During light activity, fat can provide energy at a rate fast enough to cover most of your muscles' demands. However, during more intense exercise such as climbing or sprint starts, energy must be made available to contracting muscles at a faster rate. Carbohydrate can provide such energy more rapidly than fat, and therefore it's the main fuel for intense physical activity.

A certain amount of respect should be afforded to fat, because it's an extremely efficient medium for energy storage. The body's principle reserves of fat are located under the skin, packed around vital organs, or in discrete, gender-specific fat depots. For example, men tend to pattern fat around the abdomen, whereas women tend to pattern fat around the buttocks and thighs. As a consequence of this body-wide distribution, even the leanest endurance cyclists will carry relatively inexhaustible fat reserves. The total fat reserves may exceed 100,000 calories of energy in the average cyclist, which is theoretically enough energy to complete a race as long as the 23-day Tour de France.

By contrast, the body's stores of carbohydrate contain only about 2000 calories of energy, depending upon the training status and habitual diet of the cyclist. Carbohydrate is rather inefficiently stored in muscle and the liver as glycogen. Glycogen is deposited with water in a one-to-three ratio. This high water content, although potentially useful as a small buffer against exercise-induced dehydration, greatly reduces the available storage space for energy. Thus, the body's finite stores of carbohydrate may be an important limiting factor to mountain bike performance. As such, you should give special attention to your carbohydrate intake before, during and especially after a heavy exercise bout.

The energy balance

An average cyclist can expend more than 11.7 calories of energy every minute during a race. In comparison, a cross-country runner may expend approximately 11.3 calories a minute, and a freestyle swimmer 10.8 calories per minute. However, a mountain bike racer is not your run-of-the-mill cyclist. The event is more intensely demanding than conventional road racing, from both an energy perspective, and with respect to the stresses and strains placed on the muscles, tendons, ligaments and bones. Unfortunately, there is a dearth of reliable information concerning the bioenergetics of mountain bike racing. Some provisional observations would suggest that its energy demands are more analogous to the whole-body activity of cross-country skiing, in which competitors may expend between 8.3 and 19.2 calories per minute, depending upon the phase of the race (uphill, level gliding, or downhill).

If it's assumed that a cross-country mountain bike race lasts anywhere from 90 minutes to more than three hours, the total energy expenditure may be anything from 1000 calories to more than 3000. Obviously, this absolute value will depend upon the race distance and terrain, the mass and conditioning of the cyclist, and the intensity of his or her effort.

The average daily diet provides approximately 2500 to 3500 calories of energy, along with all the other essential nutrients. Ideally, at least 60 percent of this energy should be in the form of carbohydrates (potatoes, rice, pasta), while no more than 25 percent should be in the form of fat (oils, butter, cheese). The remainder should be protein (fish, meat, egg whites, nuts and legumes). The basic diet of a mountain bike racer similarly needs to provide all the nutrients to ensure optimum health. However, a racer's total energy intake will usually need to be increased to around 4500 calories (depending upon such factors as training status, training volume, male or female, age and so on), in order to accommodate the additional demands of a very active lifestyle. It's important to stress that this increased energy intake should largely come from additional carbohydrates, rather than fats or proteins. I will return to this later in the chapter.

FUELING FOR TRAINING

No amount of high-quality training will ensure a winning performance on race day if the cyclist fails to refuel after each exercise bout. An engine just doesn't run if the gas tank is empty; the same is true of the human engine.

Refueling may begin during exercise, with an appropriately formulated drink in the water bottle. However, the greater part of refueling will take place after exercise. The post-training diet needs to be planned with the same meticulous attention to detail devoted to the actual training session. You must take time to refuel prior to further bouts of exercise. In the short term, a cyclist in energy deficit will experience a reduced training gain, and will also be more susceptible to injury or illness. But of greater concern is the potential link between an athlete experiencing a sustained glycogen-depleted state and overtraining.

TABLE 13.1 NUTRIENT CONTENT OF FOODS HIGH IN CARBOHYDRATE

	Portion Size (gr)	Energy (Cal)	Carbohydrate (gr)	Fat (gr)	Protein (gr)
Breakfast cereals					
Muesli	70	258	46.3	5.2	9.0
Corn flakes	40	147	34.0	0.6	3.4
Bran flakes	40	121	26.8	0.4	4.1
Rice Krispies	30	112	26.4	0.6	1.8
All-Bran	50	137	21.5	2.9	7.6
Milk Products					
Milk (1 pint):					
whole	488	317	22.9	18.5	16.1
2%	488	224	24.4	7.8	16.1
non-fat	488	116	24.4	0.5	16.5
Yogurt (low fat):					
natural	125	65	7.8	1.3	6.3
flavored	125	101	17.5	1.1	6.3
Bread (1 medium slice)					
wholemeal	35	76	14.6	0.9	3.1
whole wheat	35	78	15.6	0.8	3.1
white	30	70	14.9	0.5	2.3
Preserves					
honey	(per 100 gr)	288	76.4	*Tr	0.4
jam	(per 100 gr)	261	69.0	0.0	0.6
Rice (boiled)	150	185	44.4	0.5	3.3
Pasta (boiled)	230	269	59.8	0.7	9.7
Potatoes					
baked	180	189	45.0	0.2	4.7
boiled	180	144	35.5	0.2	2.5
Fruit (fresh)					
apple	150	69	17.9	*Tr	0.5
banana	150	119	28.8	0.5	1.5
orange	160	56	13.6	*Tr	1.3
Fruit (dried)					
dates (x1)	15	37	9.6	*Tr	0.3
currants (1 Tbsp)	10	24	6.3	*Tr	0.2
raisins (1 Tbsp)	10	25	6.4	*Tr	0.1
golden raisins (1 Tbsp)	24	60	15.5	*Tr	0.4
figs (x1)	20	43	10.6	*Tr	0.7
apricots (x1)	25	46	10.9	*Tr	1.2

*Tr=Trace amounts

Note: Nutrient data reproduced from iThe Composition of Foods,i by A.A. Paul and D.A.T. Southgate with permission from the authors; McCance and Widdowson: HMSO, 1978; Food Portion Sizes by H. Crawley, MAFF, 1988.

The average sports diet contains between 300 and 400 grams of carbohydrate (4.5 to 5.5 grams to one kilogram of body mass). However, this is inadequate for replenishing the glycogen stores of a mountain bike racer in regular daily training. Thus, an increased dietary carbohydrate intake of between 500 to 600 grams (8.0 to 9.0 grams per kilograms of body mass) is recommended. Cyclists following a long-term training program, or experiencing an intensive period of training, should have an intake as high as 700 grams of carbohydrate (9.0 to 10.0 grams per kilogram of body mass) in order to sustain their level of activity.

Table 13.1 provides some suggestions of high-carbohydrate foods that could be incorporated into a training diet. The energy, carbohydrate, fat and protein content are given for average servings. You should take care to ensure that any accompanying dishes are low in fat, and that the eating plan is balanced in terms of all the essential nutrients.

PREPARING FOR COMPETITION

In preparing for competition, the golden rule is never try anything new on race day. Training should provide you with an opportunity to rehearse race-day strategies, but in both training and racing special consideration should be given to your dietary schedule. The specific details of your dietary preparation for racing will need to be tailored to your personal situation, but it will generally depend upon such factors as the recovery time you're able to allow between races; the position of the event with respect to your focus for the season; and the importance with which you rate the race.

Since mountain biking is an endurance event, your performance may be improved by adopting some form of carbohydrate loading, although this may be difficult to accommodate during a busy season. Traditionalists will profess the virtues of the classic seven-day carbohydrate- loading strategy initially proposed by Scandinavian exercise scientists in the 1960s. This involves a prolonged bout of strenuous training a week prior to the race, followed by a three-day depletion phase when the athlete consumes a low-carbohydrate diet. Finally, over the four days leading up to the race, the athlete rests from training and consumes a high-carbohydrate diet. There is no doubt that this strategy does enhance the body's carbohydrate stores prior to competition, but at a price. There is always a danger when performing a hard training session as close as seven days prior to an important race, because the potential for injury at this stage

PREPARING FOR COMPETITION: ALCOHOL AND COFFEE

As a cautionary note, you should avoid beverages containing alcohol or caffeine on the eve of a race. Both alcohol and caffeine are diuretics, promoting water loss from the body. Alcohol is a carbohydrate, but its energy is not in a form that can be readily used by your muscles. Moreover, if drunk in excess it adversely affects physical performance, impairing motor control and reaction time. Caffeine might potentially improve performance, acting as a psychological stimulant on the one hand, while promoting the mobilization of fat stores on the other. However, if taken in excess, the combination of its stimulatory and diuretic effects can result in high blood pressure, irregular heart beat, tremors and migraines. And too much caffeine before a race could lead to your testing positive in an anti-doping control — anything above 5 micrograms per milliliter of caffeine in your urinalysis is considered an illegal amount by the Union Cycliste Internationale.

is relatively high, usually due to the athlete's fatigued state. Furthermore, the depletion phase may be associated with irritability, headaches, lethargy, and a poor psychological state of mind with respect to the imminent race.

During the 1980s, a more gentle approach to carbohydrate loading was shown to be equally as effective in optimizing the body's glycogen stores. It has the added advantage of not requiring the self-imposed purgatory of the classic depletion phase. The combination of a training taper (reduced training volume) with a high-carbohydrate diet (9.0 to 10.0 grams per kilogram of body mass) over the seven days prior to competition ensures that the tanks were full — and the mind set is right!

If you do wish to carbo-load, there is a side effect you should prepare for. Earlier in this chapter, I mentioned that the body deposits glycogen in association with water. So there is the possibility that you may feel heavier at the start of the race, and your muscles may feel a little stiff. The effect of this on performance may be a relatively slower start. However, this stiffness wears off during the race as you start to mobilize the glycogen stores, and you'll potentially reap your rewards later in the race as fellow competitors start to fade.

Generally, you should always ensure that your glycogen stores are well stocked during the three days prior to a race. To do this, select meals that are high in complex carbohydrates and provide the body with quality fuel as well as the requisite vitamins and minerals. In addition, you'll want to taper training to avoid drawing heavily upon these fuel reserves, and consciously increase your fluid intake to effectively over-hydrate your body.

REFUELING DURING EXERCISE

The need, and desire, to take on additional fuel and fluids during a race will depend upon the specifics of the race itself, as well as local environmental factors. The nature of mountain bike racing makes the opportunities to drink during a race minimal — if there are any at all. However, in training the constraints are not the same, and it would be wise to ensure that you refuel throughout each training session.

The most readily absorbed fuels are diluted carbohydrate solutions (6 to 8 percent), although there are now solid high-carbohydrate snacks available on the market that might be preferable during long training sessions, especially on colder days. For carbohydrate solutions, there are a number of very good energy drinks from which to chose. Those providing carbohydrate as a glucose polymer and containing a small amount of electrolytes appear to be the best. But please beware! Commercial interests can sway popular judgment. The most expensive products on the market are not necessarily the best. Don't be misled by pseudo-scientific marketing. Be wary of drinks that have a hard sell — those, for example stressing their "unique electrolytic formula." Such marketing basically refers to the salt content of the drink, and indeed electrolytes such as sodium and potassium are lost in sweat during exercise. But this loss is not sufficient to directly impinge upon performance, and a well-balanced diet can provide all the electrolytes the body needs. Nevertheless, electrolytes are important in a sports drink. Their role is to aid the passage of the drink along the gastrointestinal tract and the subsequent absorption in the small intestine. It's not necessary to instantly replace electrolyte losses incurred during the exercise bout. Once again, this replacement should take place in the diet.

Exercising in the heat brings a whole catalogue of different problems for the mountain biker. Of main concern are the problems associated with dehydration. Studies have shown that dehydration losses equivalent to 2 percent of body mass will reduce exercise performance. During 60 minutes of intense exercise in a moderate environment (68 degrees Fahrenheit), cyclists can lose in excess of 1.5 liters of sweat. Under more extreme circumstances, where the mid-summer heat may combine with a relative humidity in excess of 80 percent, this figure can increase to more than 3.0 liters. Hence, you must always view rehydration as a priority during both training and competition. Cool, relatively diluted carbohydrate-electrolyte drinks appear to be the best way to meet the body's needs in such instances. Be careful in diluting your drink, though. Providing too much carbohydrate can disrupt digestive functioning and cause intestinal distress during exercise, while delaying the rehydration process. It's also important to note that your sense of taste tends to change during prolonged exercise, especially in the heat, so that highly flavored drinks may begin to taste nauseating.

TABLE 13.2 EFFECT OF DEHYDRATION ON PERFORMANCE

Loss in Body Mass (%)	Symptoms
1	Thirst (equivalent to fluid loss of around 700 ml)
2	Impaired athletic performance
5	General discomfort: alternating states of lethargy and nervousness; irritability; fatigue; loss of appetite
>7	DANGER!! Problems with salivating and swallowing
>10	Impaired ability to walk: breakdown in coordination and spacticity
15	Delirium: shriveled skin; decreased urine volume; loss of ability to swallow food; difficulty in swallowing water
>20	UPPER LIMIT OF DEHYDRATION TOLERANCE! Skin bleeds and cracks; possibilities of infection

Note: Data from Exercise Physiology: Human Bioenergetics and Its Application, *by G.A. Brooks and T.D. Fahey, Macmillan: New York, 1984.*

RECOVERING FROM COMPETITION

The golden rule here is to start the refueling process sooner rather than later. It's been demonstrated that delaying carbohydrate ingestion post-exercise can significantly delay recovery. This in turn will delay the time when you can optimally perform again. A useful guide is that you consume at least 1 gram of carbohydrate per kilogram of body mass each hour over the immediate four to six hours following exercise.

Initially, it could be more palatable to take this carbohydrate in a liquid form. For a cyclist weighing 60 kilograms (132 pounds), this would be equivalent to one liter of a 6-percent carbohydrate solution each hour. Then, as soon as it feels comfortable to do so, eat some solid fuel. A bowl of breakfast cereal, a jam or banana sandwich are some tried and true solid snacks. Refer to Table 13.1 for the appropriate high-carbohydrate foods on which to base your recovery meal.

Should you use supplements?

It's beyond the scope of this chapter to enter into a debate over the merits (or lack of merit) of all the nutritional supplements currently on the market. In my opening comments, I suggested that the nutritional needs of an elite cyclist are qualitatively the same as the average individual, although quantitatively different. It's important that as a mountain bike racer you maintain a well-balanced diet. This is despite the added problems of training and racing on top of all the other demands on your time such as work, school or family. Supplements are usually only necessary if there is a deficiency, or if a health condition leads to some form of deficiency.

Supplementary energy in the form of glucose polymer beverages or high-carbohydrate snacks will be required to maintain the body in a positive energy balance. The daily diet should provide adequate amounts of fat and protein without recourse to powder supplements. Similarly, the diet should provide more than sufficient vitamins and minerals. However, it would be worth consulting a qualified nutritionist if you feel your diet needs to be refined to meet the needs of your active lifestyle.

As we've discussed, diet is an important part of training, one that isn't always apparent to a casual observer at a race. Another important "unseen" part of training is practicing and refining skills, which will be covered in the next two chapters.

(Author's note: This chapter on nutrition was supplied by Dr. Joanne L. Fallowfield, senior lecturer in exercise physiology at the Center for Sports Sciences, Chichester Institute of Higher Education, Chichester, West Sussex, England. She knows far more about sports nutrition than I do, and I thought you should learn from the best.)

Bibliography

Brouns, F. (1993) *Nutritional Needs of Athletes*. Wiley & Co: Chichester, UK

Clark, N. (1990) *Nancy Clark's Sports Nutrition Guidebook*. Leisure Press: Champaign IL, USA

Stanton, R. (1994) *Eating for Peak Performance*. Allen & Unwin: St Leonards, Australia

Chapter 14

Advanced downhill skills

This and the following chapter are devoted to advanced-level skills for both downhill and cross-country racing. The chapter heading, "Advanced Downhill Skills," is accurate, but the information presented here is not rocket science. Novice and less-experienced riders stand to learn the most from these tips — although they may feel intimidated just looking at the pictures. If you fall into this category, all I can say is "hang in there." After you become familiar with your bike, and get a handle on the basic skills presented in the earlier chapters, you'll probably feel like having a go at some of these more-advanced techniques.

Once you feel up to learning these skills, start practicing. If at first, you don't succeed ... stop and think about what went wrong, and then decide if it's something you want to try again. One thing worth listening to is the degree of nervousness you feel before approaching an obstacle. If the obstacle ahead makes you nervous, go find something slightly less difficult to practice on. Remember: Progression through any skill should be smooth. So, take smaller steps and avoid killing yourself. This way you'll always feel in control, or very close to it, and nervousness shouldn't be a hindrance.

If you are an advanced rider, you will probably get the most out of this chapter by thorough analysis of the photographs. For example, you might notice something about the angle of the foot, the line of vision, or the knee or hip position. For my part, I'll draw your attention to the main points, and let Missy do the rest.

PIVOTING ON A FOOT

When you come to a tight corner that you want to get around quickly, there are two basic techniques: Foot out, or foot clipped in. It's hard to say which technique is better. Observing pro riders on the super-tight switchbacks at Cap d'Ail, France, I've seen good exponents of both styles appear to be equally fast; however, those who mistimed the foot-out technique seemed to lose more time when their bike stalled. With both feet on the pedals through the corner, the bike doesn't stall unless the front end washes out, but in that case, you'll lose even more time than by stalling with the foot out! The fastest foot-out riders keep the foot planted longer and then accelerated quickly away by pushing off hard with the pivot foot. Missy demonstrates the foot-out technique in Figures 14.1-4.

PRE-JUMPING

The fastest and safest way to attack a jump is by using a pre-jump, as Missy does in Figures 14.5-10. If you haven't mastered this skill yet, take care. Missy explains why: "Pre-jumping lets you stay on the ground longer, which means you can pedal more, plus you have more control on the ground than in the air. A well-timed pre-jump actually helps you gain momentum.... But you have to be careful, because if you mistime it, and you don't lift your back end in time, and the back tire hits the lip of the jump, you're definitely going to go over the bars.

"The way you do it is to try and jump over the obstacle just before you get to it. To do this, you almost use a bunny-hop, but it's not quite the same. You have to lift your front end up first, then your back end, and place your back end down on the back side of the jump and push down — which gives you extra momentum.

"Another thing you can do on a really fast section is to try and ride the jump, and suck the bike up. The seat then comes up and hits you in the stomach." Missy displays this technique in Figures 14.11-13.

If faced with a choice between pre-jumping or absorbing the jump, the pre-jump offers a faster progress, but the absorption technique is easier to learn. Which skill you use should be determined by your confidence level. My suggestion is to practice bunny hopping until you feel super confident, and then go out and try pre-jumping. Start with smaller objects, like a water bottle on its side, and progressively tackle larger obstacles — the sky's the limit.

UNAVOIDABLE OBSTACLES
THAT COME AT A BAD TIME

The main point of this sequence is to show you that you can still attack a corner that is bisected by a water bar, rocks or

sand, as is the case in Figures 14.14-17. All you need is faith in your skills and equipment. Chances are you would feel more comfortable riding through water or sand if you were on a straight section of trail, but the fact that you are turning does create some complications. The most notable of these is that you have to approach the obstacle with slightly less speed. If you have questions about which techniques to use in a situation like

this, go back and review the pre-jump section above, and the section on **Steering and Cornering** in Chapters 2 and 11.

MANUALING

Manualing is the mountain-bike term for riding into a wide ditch. Done right, this skill can save you seconds over your competition, but it's not an easy one to master. Riding into a wide ditch sounds easy. Keeping your bike under control while you pull a wheelie and then drop into the ditch so both wheels hit the ground at the same time is a skill that requires practice and excellent balance.

Figures 14.18-20 combined with Missy's descriptions of this skill cover all the bases: "This is for the opposite of jumps — dips. You get a wheelie going, then drop the rear end into the dip, then suck the rear back up again. It's another way to gain momentum, and worth practicing, even though it's hard to do. Not only is it faster, it's also safer. If you keep the front wheel on the ground, your front end is at risk of slamming into the other side of the ditch and dumping you on your head. But if you manual, your front wheel shouldn't touch the ground until the rear one does. Just as you're about to land, you suck your rear end back up, and drop the front end down. That's it.

"You need to have your hand on the rear brakes, in case you start to go over backwards. Tap the rear brakes and that'll bring your front wheel down. It's a precaution to keep a finger on the back brake, so only use it if you need it.

"Getting the front wheel up in the first place can be difficult for women. To wheelie, you need to be strong. There is some technique involved, but the bottom line is that you need a lot of upper-body strength. That is why you see a lot of boys wheel-ieing down the street, but not a lot of girls. It's not that women aren't coordinated enough to wheelie, it's just that most of them aren't strong enough in the arms and shoulders. Remember,

women's bikes weigh just as much as men's bikes, but they (men) might weigh 180 pounds, whereas women might only weigh 130 pounds or less."

WEIGHT DISTRIBUTION

Missy advocates even weight distribution with a slight tendency to use the front wheel. This approach is common throughout downhilling circles: "I'm very even and try to stay centered on the bike. To do this, I rock back and forth a lot, but my goal is to put as much weight on the front as I do on the rear tire. If I had to make a choice about which wheel to put on the ground in most technical situations, I'd pick the front because you steer with it. You can't steer if you don't have the front wheel on the ground. The only time I go to the back wheel is when I'm in really big trouble."

SELF-KNOWLEDGE

To finish the chapter, Missy has some advice about how well you need to know a skill before you try it in a race. "Self doubt is something that you really can't have. There are times when I'm at the brink and I know I have to pull myself out, but I don't even think about pulling out, I just do it automatically." Missy's knowledge of what she can do on a bike gives her the confidence to stay loose and react without thinking.

"When I prepare for a course, I decide on the places where I'll go 110-percent. In those places I'll be beyond my limit, and it's a calculated risk. But you have to pick these areas carefully, and there are only maybe two or three per course. If you don't pick the area right, you're gonna be in trouble.

"Sometimes the course changes in between your seeding run, or your practice run, and your race. Which brings us to another reason why you need to be able to ride instinctively: To get yourself out of trouble when you don't expect it."

Practicing these advanced skills can make the difference between riding with confidence and just hanging on for dear life. Confidence is not something that can be taught; you have to find it for yourself. But once you find it, you may find that this kind of fearlessness is addictive.

Chapter 15

More cross-country skills

Finally, we come to advanced cross-country riding skills. The fact that this subject is so close to the end of the book bears no reflection on its importance. After all, finely tuned bike-handling skills are one of the most difficult aspects of cross-country riding, and therefore take the most time to learn, so it really does make sense that I've left them until last. These skills are the icing on the cake, and in terms of racing, they can save you several seconds per lap. So chances are you won't regret any of the time you spend practicing these finer points of cross-country racing.

LOW-SPEED DROP-OFF

When we photographed this sequence, Henk was unhappy with the short approach to the obstacle: "If I came into this with some speed, it would be a lot easier. Momentum would carry the bike to the lower level on a gentle trajectory…. It's not good practice to let a mountain bike fall so far on such a steep step." As an experienced racer, Henk always has his bike's welfare at the top of his priority list, whether in a race, recreational ride or photo-shoot such as ours. Needless to say, he performed four flawless drops, making a soft landing every time for the photos in Figures 15.1-3.

15.1 *Henk is just beginning his approach. He has already steadied himself on the bike, and in order to lift the front wheel, he's already stood up on the pedals a little and leaned back. We see him as he pulls his upper body up and back, bringing with it the handlebars. Note his pedal position. He has timed the front wheel raise with a firm pedal stroke, which is common practice.*
15.2 *As he goes over the lip, Henk is holding the front wheel up, but not too high. His plan is to land on both wheels at once. His body has assumed a slightly crouched position, from which he can extend to absorb the landing shock.*
15.3 *As he falls through the air, Henk drops his hands and feet. This picture shows him at the moment of impact. Notice his pedal position. This permits him to distribute his weight evenly between the pedals and keep more control over the bike. He is starting to flex his elbows and knees to absorb the impact.*

15.4-9 RIDING UP A STEP

15.4 *Henk prepares to lift the front wheel. He has assumed a neutral position for balance just before he hops up on the step.*

15.5 *Henk's style of raising the front wheel involves standing up and leaning back. This takes more upper-body strength than the seated method, but the action of raising the front wheel is still initiated by this weight shift.*

15.6 *By drawing his elbows straight back, Henk is able to put his shoulders a long way forward, thereby unweighting his rear wheel. His knees flex, coiling prior to a big hop. Notice that his pedals are in the horizontal position.*

15.7 *A controlled explosion upward from the feet (notice the pointed toes) makes it impossible for the rear wheel to stay on the ground. When the rear wheel comes up to meet the lip of the step, Henk sits down quickly in order to resume pedaling and push the wheel into the ground, which makes it keep traction with the small contact area it has with the ground. Although he explodes upward, his momentum will also carry him forward.*

15.8 *At this point, Henk sits down and resumes pedaling. If insufficient weight is placed on the rear tire now, it might slip. Throughout the movement, it's important to maintain forward momentum.*

15.9 *Safely out of trouble, Henk pedals casually away.*

The first few times you practice clearing a low-speed drop-off, it's a good idea to start out on a six- to eight-inch drop, and take a run-up so you and your bike travel far enough to completely clear the step. Having enough speed to completely clear the step usually gives you a smoother landing and lessens the chance of injury or damage to the bike.

CLIMBING A BIG STEP

As further proof that cross-country course designers are sadists, steps are often included on an uphill section of a race course. These are designed to throw a tired or less-skilled rider, just when the fatigue is really starting to set in. Once you have mastered the art of step climbing, you'll find it's easier and faster to ride these obstacles than it is to dismount and run with your bike over your shoulder. But like all mountain-bike skills, this level of riding skill doesn't happen overnight. The good news is that in a race you'll seldom need to ride up steps as big as those featured in Figures 15.4-9, but don't be surprised if you meet obstacles this big in recreational riding. In the following paragraphs, Henk describes how to ride these bumps.

"You have to get the front end up first, then, as soon as the front wheel touches down, you must move forward to put all of your weight on it to help get the back wheel up. Actually, this takes a lot of training to master. Getting the front up is the easy

part. Keeping your balance and momentum while the back comes up is more difficult.

"A curb is a good place to start. When you are ready to hop the back up, start this by bending your knees a bit then springing up. It's a jump. If you are clipped into your pedals, the back of the bike naturally wants to follow you, all you have to do is invite it along by pulling up with your knees. I don't know how those trials guys manage to jump the back of their bikes as high as they do with only platform pedals!

"It is important to practice hopping up steps over-and-over

again. That way, when you get into a race situation, you'll clear the steps without even thinking about it.

"Often you need to hop a step with very short notice, right when you least expect it. You might lose your balance slightly, especially if you are going through a rocky section. In this situation, the back wheel doesn't follow the front. You really have to put some effort into it with your legs in order to clear the obstacle."

HAIRPIN TURNS

How many times have you ground to a halt while climbing a hairpin turn? In Figures 15.10-14, Henk demonstrates the proper technique for getting around these corkscrews.

"If it is steep, always use your granny ring and pedal easily. On a steep hairpin, the front wheel gets very light near the end of the corner, and it is super easy to wash out. This is a major problem because hairpins require you to get far back on your seat for balance and power. So you really have to bend your arms and get down low over the bars. This lower posture helps put weight on your front wheel. Trying to go through a hairpin with an upright posture, you'll fail everytime. If you have taken the right line, this technique will work. But it is critical to find the right line."

This is something you have to work out for yourself. Remember that on a tight corner your rear wheel follows a smaller radius than your front wheel. If there's a steep section at the inside edge of the turn, you can help your back wheel avoid this tighter line by going wide and deep into the turn before steering into it. Also remember that on hairpins, you use less leaning and more steering to get around the corner, which is another great reason to go slower and use your granny gear for more balance and power.

"This is where your balance gets a little tricky. You might find that while trying to keep your balance, you stop for just and instant. If this happens, don't panic, just keep your position and push the pedal forward.

"In a race, it is also safer to run than to ride steep hairpins

15.10-14 TIGHT HAIRPIN
Little can be added to Henk's comprehensive explanation about riding hairpin turns. Note his wide entry line, and the wide line he maintains throughout. This is a good general rule to observe.
In figure 16.14 Henk is pretty much out of trouble, mainly due to the nature of this particular turn. On steeper, narrower turns, the bike often stalls. In this case, just hold your balance and ease the pedals back into motion. Any sudden movements would likely throw you off balance.

because the line is so critical. If you have to dismount halfway around the corner you lose a lot of time and hold up the guys behind you. That's gonna make you very unpopular."

WHEELIE

Henk's pretty eloquent on this subject, so I'll let him do the talking while you refer to Figure 15.15.

"Wheelies are not a really important skill for cross-country racers, but there's no harm in practicing them. Besides, they're fun. What is important is knowing how to get your front wheel up quickly. Being able to get the front wheel up is essential for riding over obstacles such as: logs, roots, rocks, steps and sometimes other riders. There may be times you need to lift your front wheel for several feet before you get to the object, which is where wheelie practice comes in handy."

RIDING OUT OF
A TIGHT SPOT

One of the most satisfying things you can do in a race is ride out of a tight spot that you didn't think you were going to make. It makes you want to shout, or at least sigh. Such an escape always requires delicate balance and the right amount of power at exactly the right time. In Figures 15.16-19, Henk shows exemplary style in a tight spot we found for him during our photo shoot. Notice how everything about him looks calm yet totally focused. The relaxation you see comes from confidence, while the concentration is just part of what has made Henk a world champion.

15.15 WHEELIE

15.15 *Henk prefers to stay seated for this wheelie. Notice by his grip, that he is using balance more than strength to keep the front end up. To get there, however, he had to push the front wheel down into the ground and then as the rebound came, pull hard on the bars. This movement was timed with a strong pedal stroke, and to prevent himself from going over backwards, he keeps a finger on the back brake. When performing a wheelie, application of the back brake immediately starts to bring the front end down.*

15.16-19 RIDING OUT OF A TIGHT SPOT

15.16 *From the rider's-eye-view, this is a daunting task: There's plenty to stop the rear wheel from delivering power for long enough to bring you to a complete halt. In a situation like this, you need to keep the bike moving forward. As if the rocky step was not enough, the exit after the top is also littered with stones.*

15.17 *Henk starts with a wheelie about six feet before the step. To clear the step, he uses the same technique as described earlier in the chapter.*

15.18 *Once out of the deep bowl, Henk is faced with getting his front wheel over some big rocks. He quickly pulls another wheelie. Good step-riding technique is needed here, because he must be on-balance when he starts his second wheelie.*

15.19 *With his front wheel over the rocks, Henk is pretty safe. He's already leaning forward ready to hop the rear-end up over the rocks when his back wheel hits.*

DOWNHILL RIDING

I have left most of the specific downhill skills to Missy's section of the book; however, Henk's words about downhilling make valuable reading, especially for a rider who has earned the reputation of being one of the fastest downhillers on the cross-country circuit: "You can't win a race on the downhill. Perhaps if it comes down to the last lap you can take some risks and get a slim lead. That might win you the race. But every risk you take increases your chances of crashing.

"Use the downhill to take a rest. That's the only time in a race you can rest. Full-suspension bikes allow you to relax more on the descent and catch your breath. It's a bad sign if you're still breathing hard near the bottom of the downhill. Some people go too fast trying to catch riders on the descent, then get dropped on the next climb because they don't have the energy to attack."

And, as a final word of caution, he says, "I always try to be safe on the downhill. I take as few risks as I can."

Henk takes fewer risks because he has done years' worth of work perfecting his downhill skills. In other words, the more you know, the less you have to push your limits, which is the best reason for practicing your bike-handling skills I've ever heard. Learning new skills can be a slow and frustrating process, but regardless of how long it takes, simply hang in there and keep practicing. Sooner or later the breakthrough will come. And when it does, the reward is that much sweeter if you think about the time and effort you put into everything.

That formula can be applied to almost all of racing, as well. Very soon you'll be setting your training program into full motion. The concluding chapter has a few encouraging words before you begin your journey.

Chapter 16

Closing words

At all levels, mountain bike racing is more than just a competition. It is a group of athletes using a common course in an attempt to overcome the obstacles to perfect performance. And once you get past the major obstacle of being in sound cardio-vascular shape, I think you'll find that the rest of the obstacles are internal.

In a certain sense, you should be happy that the weather, the course and your fellow competitors are out there making things difficult for you, as they should be glad that you're doing everything you can to push them beyond their limits. Only by pushing each other in this open-air arena of competition, will we ascend to new heights of achievement. If you choose to adopt this philosophy, you will emerge from each race a stronger, more-able competitor. Like Nietzsche said, "What doesn't kill me, only makes me stronger."

So embrace it all — the increased pace, the attack on the climbs, or finding out that your best time on a downhill run only puts you at the bottom of the field. Since what you resist persists, allow all these racing pressures to lift your performance to new levels, instead of getting you bogged down in the frustration of unfulfilled expectations.

Even if the pace of an attack proves to be beyond your current abilities, by jumping in and giving your all you will have gained the experience of going beyond what you previously thought you could do. So the next time you're on an attack, you'll have much more confidence in your abilities. Remember: confidence is gained by each positive experience, building one on top of another.

Another thing to remember is that there is no such thing as a bad race course. Thinking that a course is "hard" or "bad" only sets you up for failure come race time. If a course doesn't play to your particular strengths, then you've just been handed an excellent opportunity to improve some weak areas of your game. A legendary example of this approach is Henrik Djernis's memorable third consecutive cross-country championship at the 1994 world's in Vail, Colorado. In Henk's home country of Denmark, the highest elevation is less than 700 feet. Yet the base altitude of the cross-country course at Vail is over 8000 feet! Henk proved himself a truly worthy world champion there. Another example of Henk's "triumph in the face of adversity" was the previous year at Métabief, France, when the world championship course turned into a mudbath. Many of the world's finest riders talked themselves out of doing well there. But Henk just saw it as an opportunity to gain valuable experience racing in difficult conditions ... and he chalked up his second rainbow jersey in the process.

In 1995, at another muddy event — The World Cup downhill race at Åre, Sweden — Missy Giove had a similar experience. In cold, wet conditions she started with the express purpose of emerging as a more complete rider. She did that all right, and took home a handsome winner's check as well.

WINNING AND LOSING

There is nothing in the world like the feeling of winning, but the winner's podium is rarely where you learn about racing. Learning how to slide through an off-camber turn, bunny hop over a log, or descend a rutted section takes time, and comes after making mistake after mistake and then learning how to correct them. In other words, losing teaches you how to win. Very few mountain bike racers win the first race they enter — that's not why any of us got hooked on the sport.

Yet so many athletes are totally fixated on victory, as if nothing else mattered. Hardly anyone thinks of winning as presenting its own set of problems. Even though the winner may be happy to have done so well, but he or she may feel sorry for, or even contemptuous of those who have lost. This is the result of a misconception about competition, which says that "winners" are great, and "losers" are just that. Let me state very clearly that winning is not about proving yourself superior to anyone — it's about having the skills and determination necessary to be the first to cross the finish line of a given race on a given day. Who's to say that a racer who gives it his or her absolute all and finishes in the middle of the pack is any less worthy of the title of "winner" than the person who crossed the finish line first? Remember that your position at any point in the race is less important than the fact that you continuously make the most of every opportunity.

Sure, it's a pleasure and a great honor to stand on the winner's podium, but don't think for a moment that this experience is the be-all-and-end-all of sport. Regardless of what certain American football coaches have said, any athlete who believes that winning is everything is in many ways a poverty-stricken individual.

In fact, an all-consuming desire to win tends to rob you of the many pleasures that mountain-bike racing has to offer. Another problem is getting your self-esteem too wrapped up in your performance — so you're worthy of the good things in life only if you're winning. This kind of thinking usually comes from trying to fill a hole in some other facet in your life, and generally leads to all kinds of problems — as an athlete and as a human being. If you put too much importance on winning, then you'll always be tight, judging yourself every time you turn the cranks. The key to enjoying your success as a mountain bike racer is relaxing while giving it your all. Bruce Lee used this Zen approach to martial arts by calling it "fighting without fighting." The same applies to mountain-bike racing, tennis, typing, you name it. If you have a strong emotional attachment to winning, then you can't help but try too hard. This will make certain that your performance is hindered by an anxious self. (See Chapter 12.)

Placing a big emotional attachment on winning a race is caring about something that you can't control. You would do well to remember that the outcome of any race is only partly determined by your skills, your effort and your current physiology. The skills, effort and physiology of your competitors come into play, as does the course, the weather and mechanical breakdowns. So what's the point of getting so worked up about all these things you can't even control? It's far more valuable to focus your aspirations on what you know you can control: The effort you put into your own performance.

AND WHAT ABOUT MECHANICALS?

It would be wrong to leave this book without a word on that bane of mountain bikers: mechanical failure. A mechanical — as we call it — is always lurking out there, waiting to strike just when things seem to be going too well. There's only one way to deal with mechanicals: philosophically.

As Rune Hoydahl said after being deprived of the 1995 Grundig World Cup by a four-inch nail in his tire: "Oh well, that's life." And as Thomas Frischknecht said, after winning the World Cup that year partially aided by Hoydahl's bad luck, "After all the bad luck (mechanicals) I had last year, this is only fair." This is really the only logical way to deal with mechanical problems. Chances are that you'll have your share of bad luck, but it probably won't be more than your fair share. When misfortune comes your way, you'll know that you've had your dose for a while. If you feel like you are having more than your fair share of mechanicals, consider having someone else work on your bike, especially before a race. Throwing a fit every time you have a flat only makes things worse. Remember: luck (good or bad) is the crossroads of opportunity and preparation. If you want to change your luck, check and see if you have prepared as well as you think you have. American President Thomas Jefferson is quoted as saying, "I am a firm believer in luck. The harder I work, the more of it I seem to have."

As you begin or continue your mountain bike training and racing, allow me to wish you the very best of luck in this most rewarding of sports.

A p p e n d i x 1

Useful addresses

Kingcycle
EDS Portaprompt Ltd.
Lane End Road
Sands
High Wycombe
Buckinghamshire, HP12 4JQ
England
Tel: +44(0)1494.24004
Fax: +44(0)1494.37591

SRM Powercrank
Ingenieurbuero Schoberer
52428 Juelich-9
Fuchsend 24
Germany
Tel: +49(0)2463.3156
Fax: +49(0)2463.3090

American College of Sports Medicine
Post Office Box 1440
Indianapolis, IN
46306-1440
USA

American Orthopedic Society of Sports Medicine
430 North Michigan Avenue
Chicago, IL
60611
USA

IMBA
PO Box 7578
Boulder, CO
80306
USA
Tel: (303) 545-9011
Fax: (303) 545-9026

NORBA
1 Olympic Plaza
Colorado Springs, CO
80909
USA
Tel: (719) 578-4717

VeloPress/Inside Communications
(publisher of *VeloNews* and *Inside Triathlon*)
1830 N. 55th Street
Boulder, Colorado
80301
USA
Tel: (303) 440-0601
Fax: (303) 444-6788

British Mountain Biking
National Cycling Centre
1 Stuart St.
Manchester
Great Britain
Tel: +44 (0)161.230.2301

Australian Cycling Federation
68 Broadway
Sidney, NSW
2007
Australia
Tel: +61 (0)2.281.8688
Fax: +61 (0)2.281.4236

Union Cycliste Internationale
Case Postale 84
Lausanne 23
Switzerland
CH 1000

Appendix 2

The link between breathing and exertion

The sporting goods market is flooded with various devices designed to measure exertion, but one of the most effective devices for measuring exertion comes as standard equipment on most humans — your lungs.

As any rider who has huffed and puffed his or her way up a long, steep hill can testify, the amount of air an athlete needs during endurance exercise is closely linked to the level of exertion. Some experienced athletes who have been through laboratory tests, and thus identified lactate levels with particular breathing efforts, have found the frequency of their breathing to be an accurate measure of exercise intensity.

A heart-rate monitor is arguably a more accurate and reliable way to measure exertion, but if for whatever reason you are without one, breathing levels and other body signals can give you some valuable feedback. Here's how:

RECOVERY RIDES

Glide along, spinning the pedals with no feelings of leg strain. You are scarcely more aware of your rate and depth of breathing than you are when watching television. It is easy to carry on a conversation, or whistle, or sing.

LOW-INTENSITY ENDURANCE

The next level of intensity is a noticeable step up. Pedaling is by no means strained, but it does take some work. Your breathing frequency and depth have increased; although it is not what you'd call heavy. After a while, you will become aware that your breath pattern has become rhythmical, and you are pulling from the bottom of your lungs.

Conversation is relatively easy, but you will be aware sometimes of having to pull breath against the words.

HIGH-INTENSITY ENDURANCE

This is where conversation grinds to a halt. Pedaling is now dif-ficult, although nowhere near your maximum. Breathing becomes deep, and powerful. You can feel your diaphragm making a strong inspirational effort, and many riders invent a particular rhythm to make the all-important exhalation even stronger. To maintain this intensity and breathing pattern takes unbroken concentration, not to mention suffering prolonged pain.

AEROBIC POWER

Much the same as HIE, only you work fractionally harder.

LACTATE TOLERANCE

Now your legs are really hurting, and perhaps your diaphragm as well. You will, as Jane Fonda put it, "feel the burn." Your breathing is shorter, shallower and faster. It takes more of an effort. You can still maintain a breathing rhythm, but there is a strong temptation to let go and lose control of it. If you do this, however, you know you will slow down very soon after. By maintaining a breathing rhythm, you can still get enough oxygen to function until increasing lactate levels make it impossible to go on. Mr. Pain is definitely in the house, and you ask yourself questions like, "How much more of this can I take?" Some die-hard cyclists ride their lactate tolerance for as long as humanly possible, inspired by the thought that this level of masochism builds character and race-toughness.

CREATINE PHOSPHATE

One hundred-percent effort is called for here. We are talking about a short, all-out sprint, so breathing is different from normal. Some deep, full-belly breaths are good for relaxing yourself prior to a burst of effort, and for the effort itself. You will also need the oxygen after; but you will not feel the same need to control the rhythm and depth of your breathing as you have done in all the other sessions. Oxygen is not the major player in fueling this level of effort.

Appendix 3

Possible causes and signs of overtraining

PROBLEMS

Training methodology

- Too much work at or near lactate threshold
- Setting targets too high
- Increasing intensity and volume of training too rapidly
- Failure to program sufficient rest
- Insufficient refueling after training or races

Lifestyle

- Too much variation in daily routine
- Insufficient recreation time
- Interrupted or insufficient sleep
- Spreading yourself too thin
- Too many activities incompatible with cycling (parties?)
- Too many other sports

Work/school

- Exams
- Extraordinarily heavy workloads
- Problems with colleagues or fellow students
- Performance-related stress problems

Personal

- Upheavals or difficulties in family life
- Care of infant children
- Break-up of relationship

SYMPTOMS

Health signs

- Apathy
- Decrease in performance
- Elevated resting pulse (take note of anything more than 6 beats per minute over normal)
- Inability to finish training sessions or to increase pulse rate to normal highs
- Increased irritability
- Insomnia
- Lethargy
- Loss of appetite

Appendix 4

Notes on the relative difficulty of courses

If you are like most riders, there are courses you will look forward to, and others you will regard with trepidation. No doubt these feelings arise because your particular strengths are best suited to a particular type of course; for example, big guys usually do not climb as well as little skinny guys. A few years ago, a German sports scientist, Andy Jung (who has since become the head of mountain biking in the German cycling federation), attempted to grade courses in terms of objective difficulty.

Jung made a study of the total stressors on racers while competing at four different courses in the 1991 Grundig World Cup series. He did this by measuring catecholamines (a blood protein which increases the heart rate and its force of contraction). His assumption was that physical and mental stress surrounding a mountain bike race results in a higher heart rate. Jung took samples from German national team riders before the race, after the race, and after 24 hours of recovery.

He found that a relentlessly undulating course provided the toughest challenge. No. 1 on the stress charts was Houffalize; No. 2 was a tie between the city park course at Berlin, and the world championships course at Il Ciocco, Italy; No. 3 was the downhill at Kaprun, Austria.

A BRIEF LOOK AT THOSE COURSES

HOUFFALIZE is a low, undulating course, demanding good climbing and descending technique as well as excellent physical condition. There are many short, steep climbs, and few places to rest.

BERLIN is a shorter, lower, less technical course — lots of ups and downs, but they are very short and with minimal technical challenge.

IL CIOCCO is effectively a long climb and a long descent, broken up by some brief uphill sections. John Tomac was one of the only riders able to complete the entire climb without dismounting. It demands both great strength and technique. The downhill is long, undulating and technically difficult in a few places.

KAPRUN is a downhill race. In 1991, it started off with a fast, open section, moved into a mixture of technique and speed in the middle, and included more than half a mile of flat riding in deep gravel leading to the finish. The entire run took almost 15 minutes.

It is hardly surprising that Kaprun was the least stressful of the four events, particularly after a 24-hour recovery period. That race was less than 15 minutes long, compared to between two and three hours for the others. Comparing the cross-country courses, the fact that the hardest cross-country course had smaller hills requires an explanation. Houffalize, a lowland course with several short, steep hills, appears to be harder than Il Ciocco, a course in the hills of Tuscany, with long, steady climbs and descents. I would put this down to two things: that shorter descents tend to mean less recovery time; and the shorter, steeper climbs at Houffalize caused the riders to extend themselves more frequently than at Il Ciocco. So why is Berlin an easier course than Houffalize? After all, it also has short climbs. Here I think we might find the answer in the ground surface. That particular Berlin course had a sandy, smooth surface, compared to Houffalize's slippery, rooted track. Rough courses like Houffalize put extra strain on the upper body, and force the riders to make mistakes and then put in extra effort to regain their position in the race.

Technical courses with lots of hills are so difficult is because they demand almost relentless work, offer very little respite, and mistakes made on the final two laps — after riders have started to fatigue — cost a lot of extra energy.

And how would a course like Vail compare with Houffalize? Given the altitude factor, it is probably a lot harder and would demand far more recovery time.

A p p e n d i x 5

Injury limitation

Injuries resulting from mountain bike crashes serve as a sobering and painful reminder that a fun day out can sometimes turn into a family crisis.

At a sports medicine symposium held during the 1995 World Mountain Bike Championships, in Kirchzarten, Germany, analyses and figures were given by Dr. Wolfgang Schlickewei, of the University Hospital in Freiburg, Germany. His data is drawn from a study of mountain biking injuries conducted by hospitals in Freiburg and Innsbruck, Austria, between 1992-95.

The study came to the following conclusions:
The chances of serious injury or death as a result of a mountain biking crash are increased significantly by two main factors
• riding without a helmet
• riding at your usual speed in an unfamiliar area
The most common injuries mountain bikers sustain in crashes are
• broken bones
• fractured bones
• edema (bruising)
• contusions (cuts and rock rash)

Dr. Schlickewei's data showed that in the period 1992-95, the incidence of upper-body injuries increased among all cyclists — road and mountain bike. After questioning patients and relatives, the two hospitals in this study concluded that the risk of crashing increases when riding in unfamiliar terrain.

Treatment records from the two hospitals show that 100-percent more mountain bikers required hospital treatment than road riders during the survey period. Most of the mountain-bike casualties involved over-the-handlebar crashes.

Of the 3000 mountain-bike accident victims treated in the study, the location of injury is as follows:
• 3-percent spine
• 24-percent head
• 26-percent leg
• 47-percent upper body
Dr. Schlickewei also presented figures from North America that complemented his data. From a similar Southern Californian study, he showed that:
• 84-percent of mountain bike riders had been injured in a crash; 51-percent of them in the past year
• 26-percent of injuries were treated in a hospital or clinic
• 12-percent of injuries involved fractures
• 88-percent of riders were wearing a helmet; 12-percent of them received head injuries

The Southern California study's head-injury figures compare with 24-percent in the Freiburg/Innsbruck study.

Drawing on data from a five-year study made in Ontario, Canada, Dr. Schlickewei went on to discuss the 81 fatal accidents that occured in the Canadian study. In 91-percent of these fatalities, the victim had no chance of surviving. In 89-percent of these accidents, head injuries were involved. And in every case, the victim was not wearing a helmet.

Dr. Schlickewei's message was clear: Wear a helmet; ride within your limits of control; and be especially cautious when you do not know the trail or have reason to believe that the surface conditions have changed.

Appendix 6

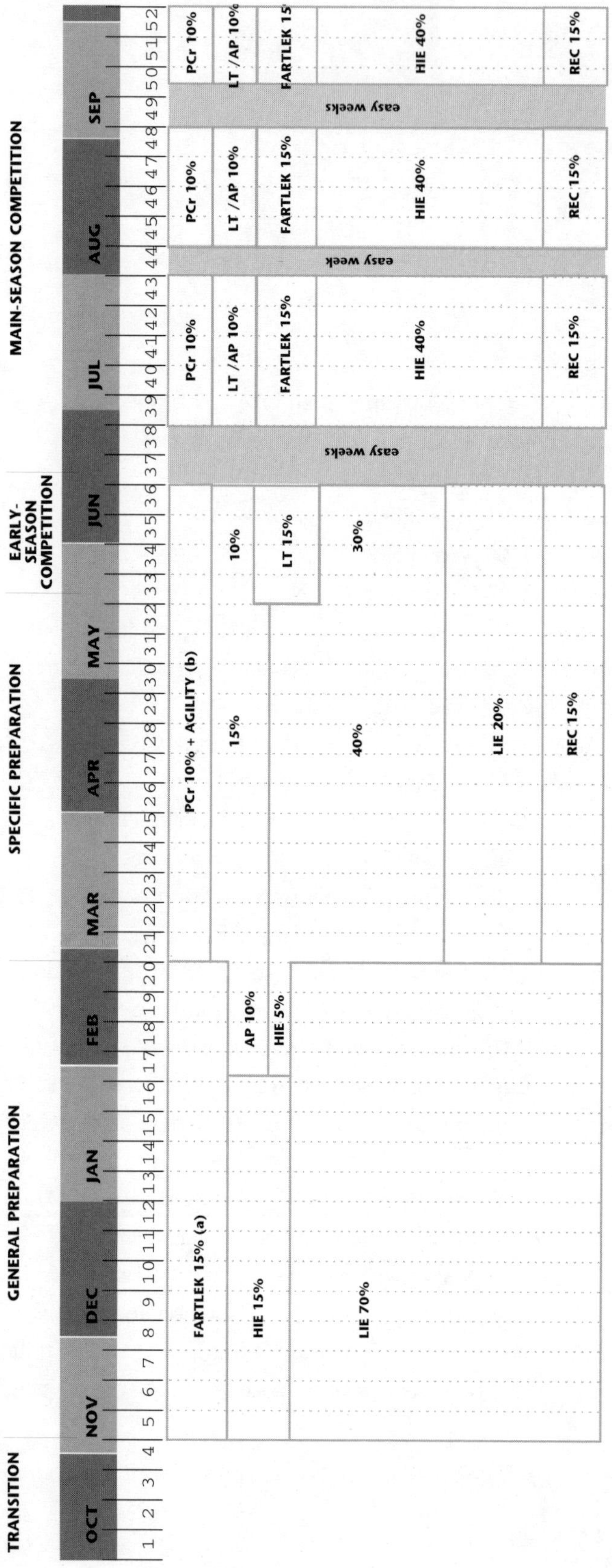

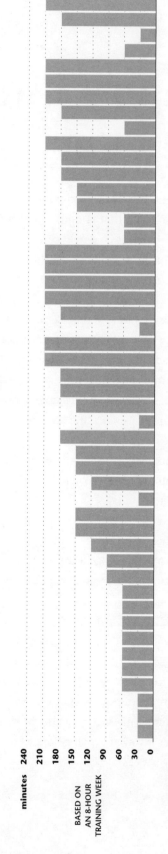

FIGURE 8.1 THE CROSS-COUNTRY YEAR LAID OUT IN TRAINING SESSIONS:
Sport Men and Women; Junior Men and Women; Veteran/Masters men and women.

FIGURE 8.2 SESSIONS WITHIN EACH PERIOD OF TRAINING, AND EXAMPLE RATE OF PROGRESS.

– 111 –

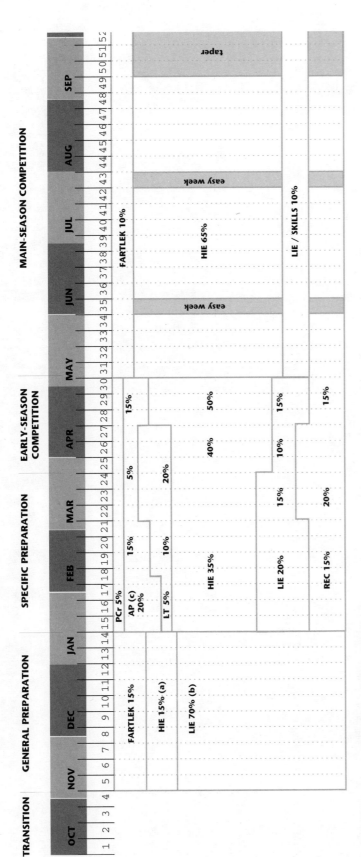

FIGURE 8.3 THE YEAR LAID OUT IN TRAINING SESSIONS:
Elite Men/Women; Expert Men/Women; some Sport riders; some Veteran Men and Women

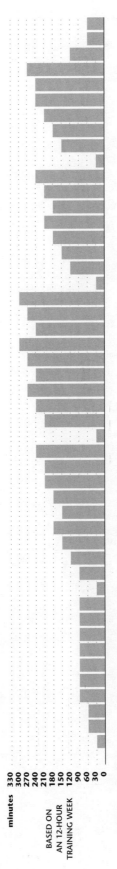

FIGURE 8.4 SESSIONS WITHIN EACH PERIOD OF TRAINING, AND EXAMPLE RATE OF PROGRESS.

A p p e n d i x 7

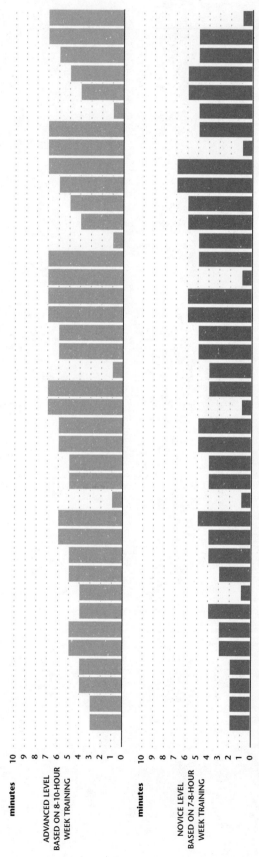

DIAGRAM 10.1 THE DOWNHILL YEAR LAID OUT IN TRAINING SESSIONS.

	TRANSITION	GENERAL PREPARATION	SPECIFIC PREPARATION	EARLY-SEASON COMPETITION	MAIN SEASON COMPETITION
	OCT	NOV DEC JAN	FEB MAR	APR	MAY JUN JUL AUG SEP

Months/weeks: OCT 1 2 3 4 | NOV 5 6 7 | DEC 8 9 10 | JAN 11 12 13 14 | FEB 15 16 17 18 | MAR 19 20 21 22 23 | APR 24 25 26 27 28 | MAY 29 30 31 32 33 | JUN 34 35 36 | JUL 37 38 39 40 41 | AUG 42 43 44 45 46 | SEP 47 48 49 50 51 52

General Preparation:
- CROSS TRAINING 30% (a)
- WEIGHT TRAINING 30% (b)
- LIE 40%

Specific Preparation:
- PCr 10%
- LT 10%
- AP 10%
- WEIGHT TRAINING 20%
- SKILLS 20%
- HIE 30%

Early-Season Competition:
- PCr 10%
- LT 10%
- AP 20%
- WEIGHTS 15%
- SKILLS 20%
- FARTLEK 20% OR CRITERIUM ROAD RACING

Main Season Competition:
- PCr 10%
- LT 10%
- AP 10%
- WEIGHT TRAINING 15% Upper body and snatch lift only
- HIE 25% Can include track racing, points racing and road criteriums
- SKILLS 30%

minutes 10 9 8 7 6 5 4 3 2 1 0

ADVANCED LEVEL BASED ON 8-10-HOUR WEEK TRAINING

minutes 10 9 8 7 6 5 4 3 2 1 0

NOVICE LEVEL BASED ON 7-8-HOUR WEEK TRAINING

DIAGRAM 10.2 SESSIONS WITHIN EACH PERIOD OF TRAINING, AND EXAMPLE RATE OF PROGRESS.

Index

AP, 33, 35-36, 58-59, 71

active recovery, 33

adenosine triphosphate, 27

ADP, 28-29

aerobic, 8, 24-25, 27-31, 33-38, 42-44, 58, 61, 72, 74, 106

aerobic capacity, 34, 43-44

aerobic power, 8, 25, 30, 34-37, 42, 58, 72, 106

alcohol, 91

amino acids, 88-89

anaerobic, 24-29, 31, 33, 35, 37-39, 54

anaerobic threshold, 24

ATP, 27-29, 31

bad habits, 86

balance, 7, 14, 21, 35, 60-61, 63-64, 67, 73, 76, 78, 89, 93, 96, 99-101

balanced diet, 88

bar ends, 12

bar width, 12

beginners, 15, 34, 38, 55, 58

berms, 49, 80, 84

bike set-up, 5, 11-12

blood lactate level, 41, 46

BMX, 5, 75

body movement, 17, 19, 84

body position, 6, 10, 13, 18-19, 63, 82, 87

brake, 11, 18-19, 66, 68, 76, 78-80, 82, 96, 101

brake levers, 18-19, 68

braking, 11, 14, 18-19, 65-66, 68, 76, 86-87

Brentjens, Bart, 24, 34

bumps, 13, 15, 17-18, 20-21, 65, 99

bunny-hop, 19, 86-87, 95

cadence, 17, 33-37, 39, 42, 46, 63

calculated risk, 97

carbohydrate loading, 91

carbohydrates, 28-30, 88-90, 92

center of gravity, 5-6, 11, 21, 77

central nervous system, 83

climbing, 36, 48, 59-60, 72, 89, 99-100, 108

club, 7, 43, 46, 48, 87

coffee, 46, 57, 70, 91

cognitive skills, 49

collarbone, 22

competition, 6, 25, 51-52, 54-56, 58-59, 70, 72, 91-92, 96, 103-104

connective tissue, 36

constant speed, 43-44

cornering, 14, 20-21, 49, 63, 65, 76-78, 82, 96

cornering technique, 21

corners, 5, 13, 21, 49-50, 80

creatine phosphate, 27-28, 38-39, 60, 73, 106

cross training, 23, 71

current situation analysis, 50, 60, 72

dangling a leg, 21

defining your mhr, 33

descending, 15, 48, 51, 62, 108

diet, 29, 41, 44, 46-47, 88-93

dietary analysis, 46

Djernis, Henrik, 6-7, 10-12, 14-22, 62-69, 84-85, 98-103

double shift, 17

downhill position, 5, 12, 15

downshift, 17

drop-offs, 14, 48-50

duration, 24, 27, 30-39, 54-55, 57, 89

ego-mind, 84

elite, 42, 55, 57-59, 70, 88, 93, 111

endurance, 23-26, 29-31, 33-35, 38, 40, 42-44, 50-51, 53-56, 58, 60, 70-73, 89, 91, 106

endurance training, 23, 25, 29, 56

energy intake, 90

energy systems, 23-24, 27, 30, 39, 54-55, 60, 73

expert, 12, 55, 59, 111

fartlek training, 38, 55

faster recovery, 36

fat, 29-30, 33-34, 46, 88-91, 93

    fats as fuel, 29

    metabolism of fat, 29

fatigue resistance, 54

feelings of intensity, 27

fitness tests, 40, 47

fore and aft, 8-9

free fatty acids, 28

front brake, 11, 18, 80, 82

front wheel control, 11

fuel, 24, 27, 29, 33-37, 39, 88-89, 90, 92-93, 105

gears, 17-18, 39, 42, 63

general preparation phase, 58-59, 71

geometry, 7

Giove, Missy, 6-8, 10-12, 15-16, 19-22, 66, 75-82, 85, 94-97, 102-103

glucose, 28, 92-93

glycogen, 28-29, 33, 35-37, 60-61, 73-74, 89, 91-92

glycolysis, 28, 31

Training notes

_____

_____

_____

_____

_____

_____

_____

_____

_____

_____

_____

Training diagrams

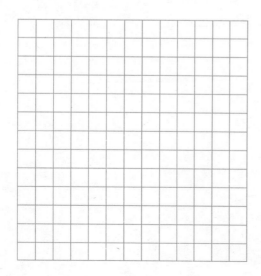 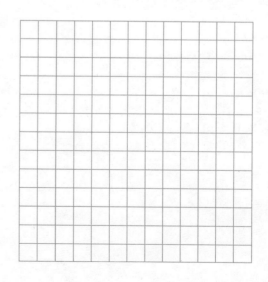

MONTH

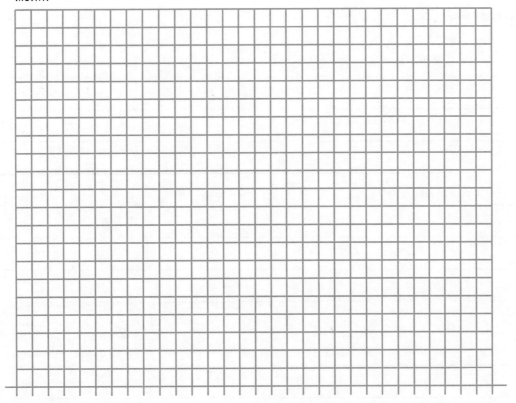

MONTH

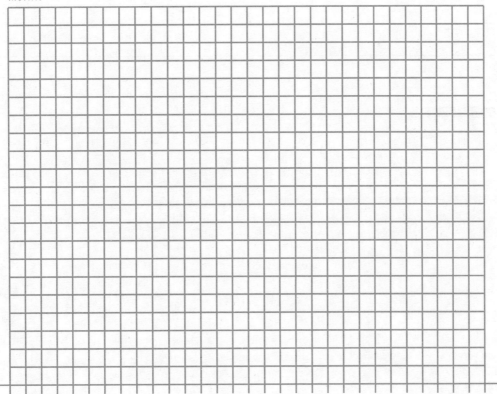

Training notes

_____

_____

_____

_____

_____

_____

_____

_____

_____

_____

_____

_____

Training diagrams

MONTH

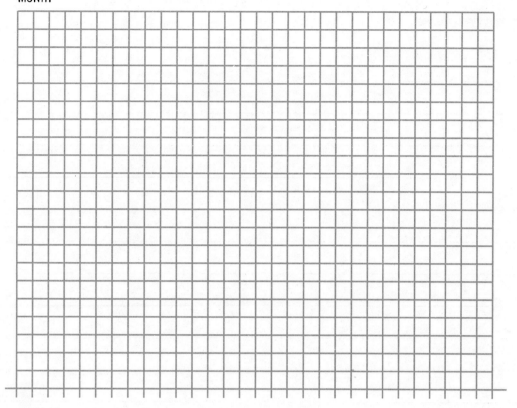

MONTH

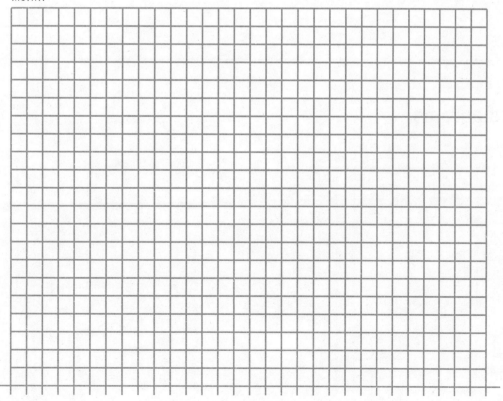

Training notes

_____

_____

_____

_____

_____

_____

_____

_____

_____

_____

_____

_____

_____

Training diagrams